Legends
OF HOCKEY

THE OFFICIAL BOOK OF THE HOCKEY HALL OF FAME

FOREWORD BY BOBBY HULL

WITH ESSAYS BY:
JIM COLEMAN, TRENT FRAYNE,
GARE JOYCE, JIM TAYLOR

PENGUIN
STUDIO

A PENGUIN / OPUS BOOK

The Renfrew (Ontario) Millionaires, circa 1909. Left to right: Bobby Rowe, Herb Jordan, Fred Whitcroft,
Edouard "Newsy" Lalonde, Fred "Cyclone" Taylor, Frank Patrick, Larry Gilmour, Lester Patrick.
All except Rowe, Jordan and Gilmour are honoured members of the Hockey Hall of Fame.

Created and produced by Opus Productions Inc.

PENGUIN STUDIO
Published by the Penguin Group
Penguin Books Canada Ltd, 10 Alcorn Avenue, Toronto, Ontario, Canada M4V 3B2
Penguin Books Ltd, 27 Wrights Lane, London W8 5TZ, England
Viking Penguin, a division of Penguin Books USA Inc., 375 Hudson Street, New York, New York 10014, U.S.A.
Penguin Books Australia Ltd, Ringwood, Victoria, Australia
Penguin Books (NZ) Ltd, 182-190 Wairau Road, Auckland 10, New Zealand

Penguin Books Ltd, Registered Offices: Harmondsworth, Middlesex, England

Opus Productions Inc., 300 West Hastings Street, Vancouver, British Columbia, Canada V6B 1K6

First published 1996

10 9 8 7 6 5 4 3 2 1

Copyright © 1996 by the Hockey Hall of Fame and Opus Productions Inc.

Printed and bound in U.S.A.

Canadian Cataloguing in Publication Data

Main entry under title:
Legends of Hockey

Includes index.
ISBN 0-670-87174-5

1. Hockey players - Biography - Pictorial works.
2 Hockey - History - Pictorial works. I. Coleman, Jim.

GV846.5.L44 1996   796.962'092'2   C96-930782-9

Front double endsheet: An open-air hockey game featuring the Montreal Victorias, circa 1895.
Hall of Famer Graham Drinkwater is foreground, second from right. Front single endsheet: Members of the
Listowel Hockey Club, Ontario Hockey Association Intermediate Series Champions, 1898.

Table of Contents

Foreword

When I was about 10 years old, Mom and Dad took me to Maple Leaf Gardens, where we stood behind the blues to see the Leafs play the Red Wings. It was actually my second NHL game. The first time the Rangers were there, and we stood in the freezing rain for two hours so we'd be sure to get in and have a place to stand. But I remember the Detroit game best, because I got to meet Gordie Howe and Ted Lindsay. We'd been waiting in the lobby, because my Dad seemed to know that the players had to go that way to catch the train. First Gordie came out—Holy Dinah, that was something!—then Ted. Dad tore the top off his pack of Export A, dug out a stub of pencil and said "Robert, go over and get Gordie's autograph."

"No way," I said. But I saw kids coming away with their heads still on their shoulders, so I ventured over and said "Mr. Howe, can I please have your autograph?"

"Sure, son," he said—and tousled my hair! Gordie Howe signed that cigarette box top— and tousled my hair! When Ted Lindsay came out, I was so excited I went up and asked him if I could have his stick. "I'd give it to you, son, but I promised it to someone down at the railroad station." And away they went.

Eight years later I was playing against Gordie Howe and with Ted Lindsay, who came over to the Blackhawks in 1957, the year I broke into the NHL. What a thrill! They weren't my only heroes. How could they be when we grew up listening to Foster Hewitt doing the Leafs games? But they were two of the greatest players in the game, and they'd stopped and spoken to me, and I had Gordie's autograph. Or, rather, my Dad did. I think he wore out that cigarette box top, hauling it out of his wallet to show people Gordie's signature. You don't have to be a kid to have heroes.

This book is about many of the legends who built the game, who signed their names and tousled the hair of kids who dreamed the dreams that they too had dreamed. The game is bigger now, but it will never be bigger than a small boy's dreams.

—BOBBY HULL, August 12th, 1996

On the frozen shallows of the Bay of Quinte, a six-year-old Bobby Hull takes a break from an endless game of shinny to smile for the camera.

Part One

LORD STANLEY'S LEGACY

1893 — 1917

As governor-general of Canada, Frederick Arthur Preston, Baron Stanley of Preston, viewed seriously his responsibility of unifying the still-new Dominion. Thoughtfully, he had observed the passion with which two of his sons, Arthur and Edward, embraced the game of ice hockey. What better way to engage the country in common purpose than to create a trophy recognizing athletic excellence in its national winter pastime? In this way, the Dominion Hockey Challenge Cup — known to posterity as the Stanley Cup — came into being. The Cup was first presented to the Montreal Amateur Athletic Association's hockey team in 1893, as champions of the Amateur Hockey Association of Canada, and for a time it would remain a challenge trophy, open for contention by whatever team issued a challenge to the incumbent champion. Over the next decades, across North America, towns and cities great and small, from Montreal to Seattle, Rat Portage to New Glasgow, put in their bids to claim the trophy. In its pursuit, the nation's best athletes would be transformed from mere mortals into legends of the game of hockey.

Facing page: *A fundamental irony surrounds Lord Stanley, the man who donated the trophy that has become the Grail sought after by all hockey players. The affable nobleman returned home to England without having seen a single Stanley Cup game.*
Previous pages: *A match between two Montreal teams, the Victorias and the AAAs, Victoria Rink, Montreal, 1891.*

Lord Stanley.
Gov Gen

The Montreal Amateur Athletic Association team of 1893 was the first
to be presented with Lord Stanley's trophy. They were forced to relinquish
it to their Montreal rivals, the Victorias, champions of the
Amateur Hockey Association, in 1895.

An exceptionally talented multi-sport athlete, centre ice man Donald H. "Dan" Bain
(seated, front row left) scored three goals in the Winnipeg Victorias' 1896 Stanley
Cup challenge triumph over the Montreal Victorias. Bain later coached the
Winnipeg squad to Cup victory in 1901 against the Montreal
Shamrocks. Whitey Merritt (seated, front row right) wore
cricket pads when tending goal.

Top: *Lester Patrick (front row, far left, with The Montreal High School Hockey Club of 1899–1900) quickly accomplished what, for most hockey men, would have been sufficient, winning two Stanley Cups on defence with the Montreal Wanderers in 1906 and '07.* Bottom: *The Montreal Shamrocks of 1899, with future Hall of Famers Art Farrell (far right), Fred Scanlon (seated, second from left) and Harry Trihey (seated, third from left) on their roster, successfully challenged the Queen's University team for the Stanley Cup.*

Facing page: *Seen here in the colours of his hometown Pembroke, Ontario, team, Frank Nighbor went on to a long and distinguished professional career. He was the inaugural winner of the Hart Trophy as most valuable player in 1923, and the Lady Byng as most gentlemanly player in 1925. Over his career, Nighbor shared in one Stanley Cup victory with the Vancouver Millionaires, in 1915, and in all four of the Ottawa Senators' Cup triumphs in 1920, '21, '23 and '27.*

Percy LeSueur was in the nets for three of Ottawa's Stanley Cup victories:
in 1906, '09 and '11, then switched to the Toronto Shamrocks in 1914. Two years
later he donned a soldier's uniform, serving overseas with the 48th Highlanders.
Returning from war, he did not play again, but stayed close to hockey
as a sportswriter and broadcaster.

The glorious "Silver Seven" from Ottawa vanquished all comers in Stanley Cup contention from March 1903 through February 1906. Sparkling at centre and rover was "One-eyed" Frank McGee (standing, far right). He had reportedly lost his eye to an errant stick's butt-end. In one Stanley Cup challenge match against Dawson City on January 16, 1905, he scored an unmatched record 14 goals—eight in little more than eight minutes—to lead his team to a 23–2 victory. Other Hall of Famers pictured include Harry Westwick (standing, far left), Billy Gilmour (standing, centre), Harvey Pulford (seated, second from left) and Alf Smith (seated, second from right).

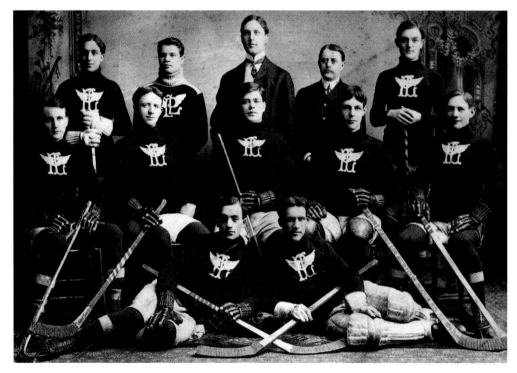

Top: *Captain of the Montreal AAA team that successfully defended the Stanley Cup in February of 1903 was R. R. "Dickie" Boon (third from left, second row). Dubbed one of that team's "Little Men of Iron" at 118 pounds, Dickie Boon was a defenceman who used his speed and finesse to elude larger opponents. In 1910, with Boon as coach, the Monteal Wanderers became the first champions of the National Hockey Association.*

Bottom: *A painless dentist by profession, and a punishing defenceman by avocation, John L. "Doc" Gibson (centre, second row) formed his own league in 1903 when he was banned from playing in the Ontario Hockey Association for accepting payment: the International Professional Hockey League— North America's first professional league—which included his team, the Portage Lakes. (Hall of Fame brothers William Hodgson "Hod" Stuart and Bruce Stuart are at the right of the second row.)*

It just would not have looked right: "Rat Portage—Home of the Stanley Cup."
Twice in the first decade of the 20th century, the Thistles, from the small
Ontario town of Rat Portage, challenged for the Stanley Cup; twice they lost. Then,
in January 1907, after the town changed its name to Kenora, the Thistles were
triumphant. Their glory was fleeting, though. In March of the same year, the
Montreal Wanderers, from whom the Thistles had won the trophy, wrested it back,
and Kenora never again was a contender. On the Cup-winning Thistles were Hall
of Famers Joe Hall (top row, far right), Tom Hooper (centre row, second from left),
Tom Phillips (centre row, second from right), Billy McGimsie (centre row, far
right), Si Griffis (front row, far left) and Art Ross (front row, far right).

Cyclone Taylor

Frederick Wellington "Cyclone" Taylor was nicknamed by His Excellency, Earl Grey, the governor-general of Canada. When Ottawa's new Dey's arena opened with a home game against the Montreal Wanderers on January 11, 1908, Lord Grey and his daughter, Lady Sybil, occupied front-row seats in the crowd of 7,100. Taylor, in his first appearance on Ottawa ice, scored four goals from his defence position as the Senators routed Montreal, 12-to-2.

Cyclone Taylor began his major league career in 1907 with the Ottawa Senators of the Eastern Canada Amateur Hockey Association. In 1909, as ECAHA champions, the Senators, with Taylor on defence and Percy LeSueur in goal, were awarded the Stanley Cup. Bruce Stuart, Marty Walsh, Percy LeSueur, Billy Gilmour and Cyclone Taylor have all since been inducted into the Hockey Hall of Fame.

The governor-general had become a keen hockey fan since he arrived from England four years earlier. As he left the arena with Lady Sybil that night he said quite loudly: "That new number 4, Taylor; he's a cyclone if I ever saw one." Malcolm Brice, of the Ottawa *Free Press*, overheard the governor-general's remark and he reported it, verbatim, in the next morning's newspaper. Fred Taylor wore the nickname proudly until he died 72 years later, at the age of 96.

Fred Taylor richly deserves his place as one of hockey's most enduring legends. No one knows how many goals he scored in his early years because existing record-books list only the statistics for 14 seasons in which he played for Ottawa, Renfrew and Vancouver. However, in those 14 years, he scored 194 goals in a total of only 186 league games.

Fred was born in Tara, Ontario, but he grew up in nearby Listowel. His father, Archie, had to scratch for a living, supporting a wife and five children on the tiny salary he earned as a travelling salesman for a farm machinery manufacturer. The Taylors couldn't afford toys for their children. Fred's first pair of skates was a gift from Jack Riggs, the Tara town barber.

Taylor was short and stocky—only five feet, eight inches tall. But, after he received those gift skates from the town barber, it was evident immediately that he was destined for hockey stardom. When Norval Baptie, the world speed-skating champion came to Listowel, he taught Fred the art of backward skating. By the time that Taylor turned professional, even his most envious rivals conceded that he was the swiftest, most agile and most versatile skater in hockey.

Fred was raised in a home of church-going Methodists. Although hockey brought him into contact with some boisterously uninhibited playmates, he went through his entire life without taking a drink, smoking a cigarette or playing a game of cards. And he never swore—at least not publicly.

But he was as tough as pemmican. Opponents soon learned to treat him with caution because he could administer a sturdy poke-check in the ribs or give a rival a clout across the chops with his hockey stick. And opponents were careful to refrain from joshing Taylor about his receding hairline. He became almost completely bald when he was in his 20s.

He left home at 20 to play hockey in Portage La Prairie, Manitoba. He received his room and board, plus $25 per month pocket money. But this move gave him his first opportunity to play against Edouard "Newsy" Lalonde, Lester and Frank Patrick, Si Griffis and Tom Phillips, who were scattered around the Manitoba League and neighbouring Federal League.

He became an outright professional in 1906 when he accepted $400 and living expenses for playing a half-season for the Portage Lake Club in Houghton, Michigan. Most of his teammates were Canadians, and four of them—Riley Hern, Joe Hall and Bruce and Hod Stuart—became members of the Hockey Hall of Fame.

However, the International Professional League folded after two seasons and Taylor found himself being wooed avidly by the Ottawa Senators, who offered him $500 for a 10-game season, plus a job in the Canadian Civil Service at $600 per year. Fred spent two seasons with the Senators and, in 1909, they won the Stanley Cup. Then, quite suddenly, Taylor became the most publicized athlete in Canada.

John Ambrose O'Brien, a mining tycoon, got together with the Montreal Wanderers to form their own professional league, the National Hockey Association of Canada. O'Brien announced that he wanted Cyclone Taylor to be the centrepiece for his Renfrew team. O'Brien landed Taylor by paying him $5,250 for a single two-month season of only 12 games, and the entire amount was deposited in Taylor's Ottawa bank account before the first game was played.

The Renfrew lineup was impressive. The goalie was Bert Lindsay, father of Ted Lindsay. Frank Patrick and Cyclone Taylor were the defence. Lester Patrick played rover. Herb Jordan was the centre and his wingers were Bobby Rowe and Larry Gilmour. Even the celebrated Newsy Lalonde was induced to join them.

At the end of their second season, O'Brien's league folded. In the scramble to grab the Renfrew players, the Montreal Wanderers claimed the rights to Fred Taylor. Fred Taylor refused to budge. He vowed that he wouldn't play hockey if he didn't play for Ottawa. The league was just as stubborn as Taylor. He was suspended from professional hockey for the entire 1912 season.

An extraordinary agility and swiftness on his skates, joined with a supreme confidence
in his ability, served Cyclone Taylor well throughout his 15 seasons in hockey.

Resultantly, Cyclone Taylor made a lifetime move to Vancouver. Backed by their lumberman father, Lester and Frank Patrick had built Canada's first artificial ice arenas in Victoria and Vancouver. They formed their own Pacific Coast Hockey Association with New Westminster as the third franchise. Frank Patrick managed the Vancouver Arena, which accommodated 10,000 spectators. It was, next to New York's Madison Square Garden, the largest sport building in North America.

In 1913, Frank signed Cyclone Taylor to the Vancouver Millionaires for a salary of $1,800. The Patricks had political connections and they arranged for the Immigration Department to move Taylor's job to Vancouver, with his salary raised to $1,200 annually.

Taylor had 10 great seasons in Vancouver, surrounded by such celebrated teammates as goalie Hugh Lehman, Mickey Mackay, Si Griffis, Frank Nighbor, Frank Patrick and Barney Stanley. The Millionaires won the Stanley Cup in 1915, scoring a three-game sweep of the Ottawa Senators.

When he was 35, in 1918, Cyclone led the PCHA in scoring with 32 goals in an 18-game schedule. He led the league again in 1919, when he was 36. He retired in 1921, then came back to play one game in 1923, when he was 40.

Hockey's most durable legend—that Cyclone Taylor skated backward through an entire team and scored a goal—originated in 1910, the night before Taylor and the Renfrew Millionaires played their first game in Ottawa.

Taylor and Ottawa goalie Percy LeSueur were joshing in the sports department of the Ottawa *Citizen.* Taylor said, good humoredly: "Tomorrow night, I'll score a goal by skating through the Ottawa defence, backward." An alert reporter plastered Taylor's remark in the next morning's edition of the *Citizen.*

Taylor didn't score a goal of any type against Ottawa in that particular game. However, three weeks later, the teams met again in Renfrew. According to Eric Whitehead who wrote Taylor's authorized biography, "Fred the Showman stole the puck, sped down the boards through the Ottawa defence, wheeled around, skated backward for the lasts few strides and flipped a backhand shot past the startled LeSueur."

Taylor (second from right, back row) ended his career

playing alongside Frank Nighbor on the Pacific

Coast Hockey Association's Vancouver Millionaires,

where he won another Cup in 1915, the Millionaires

beating the Senators in three straight games.

The guiding genius of the Millionaires—as owner,

manager, coach and occasional defenceman—was

Frank Patrick (front row, centre).

Top: *The Vancouver Millionaires—in fact the whole PCHA—were the brainchild of Frank Patrick and his brother Lester, who built rinks in Vancouver and Victoria, hired the best talent available, like Edouard "Newsy" Lalonde (second from left), then challenged the eastern hockey powers for supremacy. A five-time winner of the NHA scoring title, Lalonde won the Stanley Cup with the NHL's Montreal Canadiens.*

Bottom: *Seated behind the mascot of the 1912–13 Cup-winning Quebec Bulldogs is their captain, "Phantom" Joe Malone. Malone was a leading scorer in the National Hockey Association's last years, then led the fledgling NHL in its first season, 1917–18. On January 31, 1920, he put seven pucks past a shell-shocked Ivan Mitchell in the Toronto net.*

Top: *The Montreal Wanderers held the Stanley Cup four times from 1906 through 1910. Art Ross (far left, front row) would later jump to accept a rich offer from the Haileybury Comets of the NHA in 1909. He later became, for 16 seasons between 1924 and 1945, coach of the Boston Bruins, while at the same time serving as the team's general manager for 30 years until 1954.*

Bottom: *The Hall of Fame lineup of the 1913 Toronto Blueshirts included Harry "Hap" Holmes (far left, back row), Frank Nighbor (third from left, back row), Allan "Scotty" Davidson (far left, middle row), Harry Cameron (centre, middle row) and Frank Foyston (second from right, middle row).*

Above: *The outstanding American-born player of his time, Hobart "Hobey" Baker was captain of the collegiate champion Princeton University Tigers. When the United States entered World War I in 1917, Baker signed up. He died when his fighter plane crashed in France in 1918. Baker's contribution to hockey is still recognized through the award that bears his name, presented annually to the top American college hockey player.*

Facing page: *James Dickenson "Dick" Irvin was a member of the Portland Rosebud team that took Georges Vezina and the rest of the Montreal Canadiens to five games in the Stanley Cup challenge of 1916 before losing—the first American team to compete for the Cup. One year later, Irvin was in uniform. Resuming his high-scoring career in 1921, he played in Regina and Portland with the Capitals, then joined Chicago in 1926 as captain.*

Part Two

BIRTH OF THE NHL
1917 — 1931

*T*he turn of the century had seen many new hockey leagues spring to life, then wither and die as their founders' dreams ran headlong into reality. When the National Hockey Association, lacking clear direction, ceased operations in 1917, representatives from its surviving franchises—the Ottawa Senators, Montreal Wanderers, Montreal Canadiens and Quebec Bulldogs, along with Frank Calder, who had been secretary-treasurer of the NHA—gathered in a room at Montreal's Windsor Hotel. Their goal, in their words: "to ascertain if some steps could not be taken to perpetuate the game of hockey." Their solution: the National Hockey League. From its Canadian birthplace, the league would expand to embrace communities in the United States. Its name would become synonymous with excellence in hockey. Some of the most enduring legends of the game would be born—names like Vezina and Joliat, Foyston and Holmes. A national pastime would become a continent-wide passion, and an exalted standard of play would be set against which all hockey players who followed in their footsteps would be measured.

Previous pages: *The star-studded lineup of the 1921–22 Montreal Canadiens was led by their forceful coach and manager, Léo Dandurand (fourth from left). Facing page: Such was the appeal of the honour of winning it that, by the mid-1920s, space on the Stanley Cup to inscribe names of winning teams and players was becoming scarce.*

On November 22, 1917, at the Windsor Hotel in Montreal (top), team representatives from Toronto, Ottawa, Quebec and Montreal met to decide upon their fate. The National Hockey Association was in tatters, and had suspended operations. Confident in the future of hockey, they took an historic leap of faith and established the National Hockey League. The firm hand of President Frank Calder (bottom) shaped the National Hockey League's destiny over its first quarter-century.

GEORGES VEZINA

His name now immortalized through the trophy awarded annually to the NHL's best goaltender, Georges Vezina,
"The Chicoutimi Cucumber," coolly distinguished himself through 15 seasons in the nets with the Montreal Canadiens
of the NHA and NHL, from 1910 until his death from tuberculosis in 1926. For the 1923–24 and
1924–25 seasons, in his mid-30s, Vezina recorded the league's best goals-against
average with 1.97 and 1.81, respectively.

As the era began, the Stanley Cup was still a challenge trophy, won for the first time by an American team in 1917 when the Seattle Metropolitans beat the Montreal Canadiens. On Seattle's roster were future Hall of Fame forwards Jack Walker (fourth from left) and Frank Foyston (sixth from left), and goaltender Harry "Hap" Holmes (far right).

Frank Foyston scored four goals in seven games on Seattle's 1917 playoff road
to the Stanley Cup. Foyston already had his name on the Cup once, as a member
of the 1913–14 Toronto Blueshirts, and in 1925, he repeated his triumph,
helping the Victoria Cougars of the Western Canada Hockey League
to a Cup victory over Montreal.

A veteran of the Royal Flying Corps in World War I, Frank Frederickson
(fifth from left) stands with the Winnipeg Falcons, Canada's 1920 Olympic gold-
medal-winning hockey team. Frederickson carried his talents to the Victoria Cougars,
where he won the PCHA scoring title in 1923 and the Stanley Cup in 1925,
before trying his hand as a playing coach of the new
Pittsburgh Pirates of the NHL.

The purity of the amateur game attracts a dedicated few. Like Hobey Baker before
him, Harry "Moose" Watson proved that the best hockey players were not necessarily
found in the professional ranks. A star left-winger with Canada's 1924 Olympic
hockey champion Toronto Granites, he sparked the team to a series of lopsided
victories, culminating in a 6–1 triumph over the Americans. Watson
rejected lucrative offers to turn pro, retiring instead.

Across the nation, the promise of fame and fortune inspired young men to venture into the game of hockey. A young Clint Smith, seen here (second from left, centre row) with his Assiniboia, Saskatchewan, junior team, would be one of the fortunate and talented few to go on to the NHL. Smith starred with the 1939–40 New York Rangers: the last Ranger team to win a Stanley Cup for more than half a century.

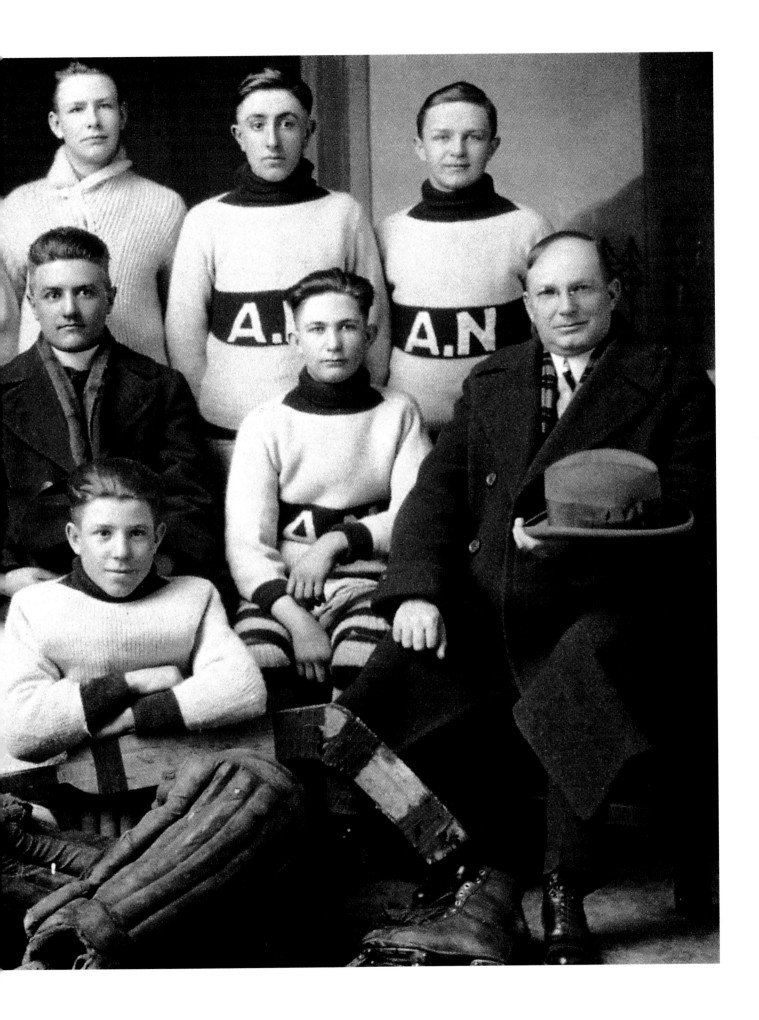

Foster Hewitt

oster Hewitt, who broadcast the first hockey
game ever carried on radio, the first ever carried
on network television, and the one from Moscow
in 1972 that every living human in all of Canada
listened to (give or take a newborn babe), was a shy,
unassuming man who had a front row seat at sports
events for even longer than he could remember.
His father, W. A. (Billy) Hewitt, was the sports editor of
the *Toronto Star* when Foster was growing up.

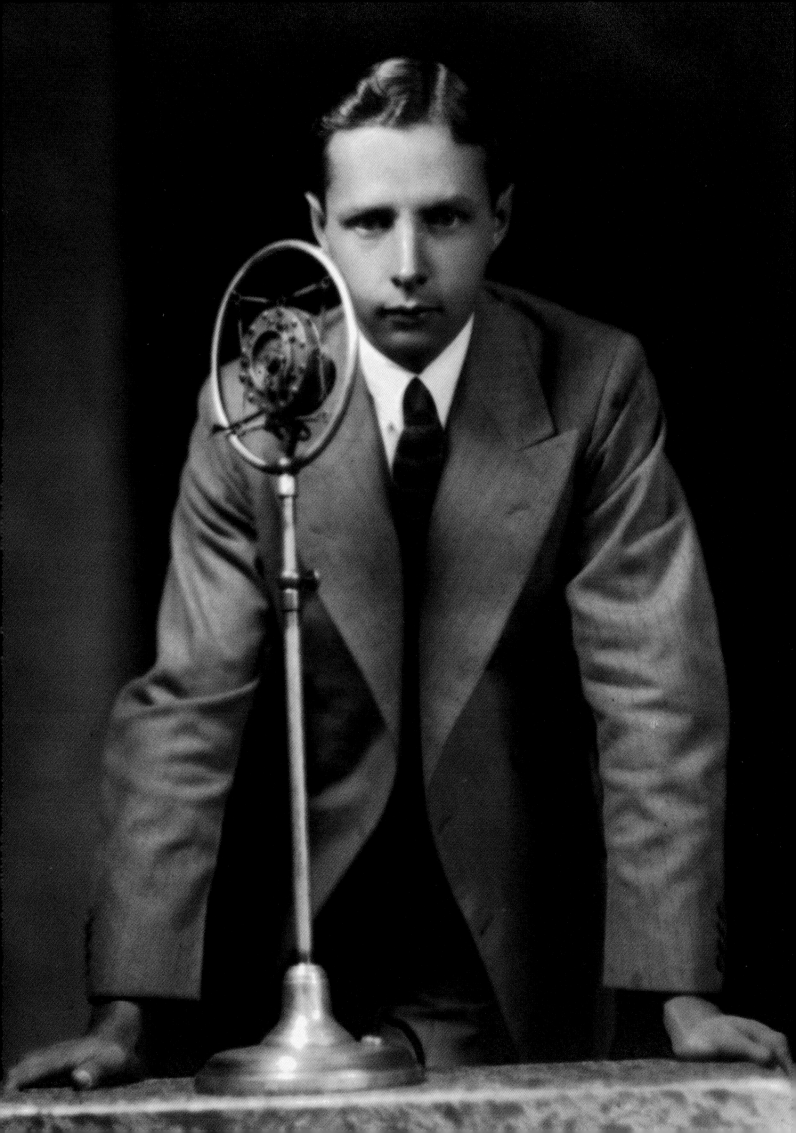

To C.C.M. hockey fans with best wishes

Foster Hewitt

For more than half a century, starting on March 22, 1923, Foster Hewitt cast a magic spell that mesmerised all of Canada. Broadcasting Toronto Maple Leafs games from the old Mutual Street Arena and, as of 1931, from Maple Leaf Gardens, he painted word pictures that embellished the legends of the National Hockey League. Even as a young man, Foster Hewitt enjoyed a celebrity that matched, and at times exceeded, that of the players whose play he so poetically described.

Billy Hewitt often took his boy along on assignments. Foster accompanied his father to New York when he was two, saw a hockey game in Madison Square Garden when he was three, and at 10 he shagged flies occasionally in the outfield of the old Toronto Maple Leafs baseball club.

In 1921, when Foster was 18, Billy took him to Detroit so he could hear radio for the first time. He listened on a crystal set to the legendary baseball player Ty Cobb talking and was so fascinated that he bought 50 crystal sets and took them home to sell. Not everyone shared his enthusiasm. "It took me two years to get rid of them."

As a boy he was quiet and neat and a loner. When he was not with his father or at school he played by himself at home. The floor of his third-floor room was covered with boys' toys—an electric train that he kept tuned to the minute, and brigades of miniature toy soldiers—Highlanders, Arabs, boy scouts—numbering more than 1,500.

He and his father were always close—his sister, Audrey, was more closely attached to their mother—and even in later years, when Billy Hewitt was in his mid-80s, he lived with Foster's family of two girls and a boy in a 14-room home in the fashionable Rosedale section of Toronto.

The Hewitts were a closely knit bunch. Foster's first name was derived from his mother's maiden name. Foster's son Bill was named Foster William Alfred after his father and two grandfathers; Bill's son was named Bruce after his maternal grandfather and was also named Foster William. Foster's daughters, Ann and Wendy, named *their* daughters for each other.

Foster had an arrangement with Conn Smythe, the boss at Maple Leaf Gardens, that gave him exclusive broadcast rights in the big new arena. No one other than Foster could broadcast from his famous gondola, except son Bill, who eventually succeeded him as the Maple Leaf's broadcaster, and Bill's son Bruce, whom Bill brought in occasionally to handle part of the hockey broadcast during the annual Young Canada Night. As June Callwood observed in a *Maclean's* magazine article, "The Hewitts have a long bench."

When Foster Hewitt sat down in front of the microphone, the players below his gondola were nine feet tall. This wasn't particularly because of his choice of words or because he was a homer, though hundreds if not thousands of non-Leaf's fans believed he was, as much as it was because of his style. From the outset he spoke forcefully, even deliberately, letting his voice reflect the flow of play, rising and falling on the mood of the crowds. Since he broadcast Toronto games, the excitement level was highest when Toronto had the puck, and Hewitt's voice turned to its highest pitch when the home town Maple Leafs scored a goal. Then came the familiar cry: "He shoots! He *scores!*"

"No one taught it to me or suggested it," he said once of this signature. "It just seemed the best way to describe it."

Mostly he used plain, worn words, some of them clichés, and he had an oft-repeated gaffe. "The crowd literally raised the roof," he'd say of a high moment. Even so, the trenchant tones of an evangelist captivated listeners. He could accentuate the positive, eliminate the negative. He didn't bother describing play or identifying players when the game was scrambly and the passes errant. He'd fill with sidelights until play became organized. Then he'd leap into the specifics. He had an uncanny sense of an impending goal, his voice invariably beating the crowd's roar. "Nobody else could bring to hockey the excitement, the love, the awe," Scott Young wrote of him. "It was a gift."

Away from the microphone Hewitt was a self-effacing man, his manner shy. He wasn't big, five foot eight perhaps and 150 pounds, but he was no Casper Milquetoast. He'd been a boxing champion in high school and at the University of Toronto, and early on was disappointed that he wasn't heavy enough to succeed as a professional athlete.

"It all worked out for the best." he said later. "I am very happy now that I didn't do better in sport. I was guided into being an observer rather than a participant, the most fortunate thing that ever happened to me as far as my career is concerned."

Soon after graduation Foster got a job at the *Toronto Star* as a court reporter. Years later, this aspect of his career was a source of pride for his father. "He wouldn't take a job in the sports department," beamed Billy. "He wouldn't let me help him."

After a month covering the courts, Foster was assigned to look after a radio column and occasionally

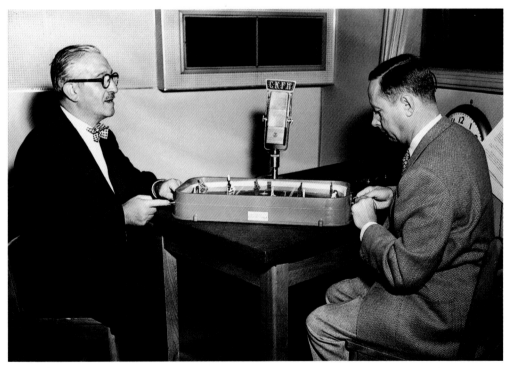

Top: *With star-struck fans from Upper Canada College looking on, Hewitt interviews Leafs hero Syl Apps.*
Bottom: *Hewitt engages an opponent in an early version of table hockey—this one was personally endorsed by Hewitt himself.*

go on the air for the paper's radio station, CFCA. In 1923, the *Star* began live broadcasts of local events and one night assigned the cub reporter Hewitt to a hockey game at Toronto's Mutual Street Arena, the first game ever covered on radio. "I had no idea how to do it since it had never been done, but I was willing to try," Hewitt said years later. "It was a crucial local game, so away I went to the arena."

The broadcast facilities were spartan. His booth was a vertical box, resembling a telephone booth, installed in the penalty box. It was air tight, so Hewitt had to keep opening the door to get a breath of fresh air and wipe steam from the window so he could see. It had a window and was four and a half feet high. A quarter of a century later his most vivid recollection of that first broadcast experience was still a trifle exasperated: "The game went into overtime."

After that, he did all the sports that his masters could dream up for the radio station, and some of his impromptu locations were even more trying than the hockey booth. He broadcast a football game between his alma mater, the University of Toronto, and Queen's University in Kingston, Ontario. His perch was precariously pitched on the stadium roof, which the crew reached by climbing a ladder with heavy equipment on their backs. Hewitt positioned himself with his heels in the eavestrough while an operator in a safer position kept a firm grip on a wire wound around Foster's body in the unlikely event it would save his life if he skidded off.

In 1931, the year Maple Leaf Gardens opened, the *Star* gave up CFCA. Hewitt's father left the paper to become attractions manager at the new Maple Leaf Gardens and urged his son to do likewise. Three years earlier Foster had demonstrated the popularity of the broadcasts; he mentioned on the air that if listeners sent a dime to the station they'd receive a copy of the small Maple Leafs hockey program. The response was so large that Hewitt believed it sold Smythe on the value of hockey broadcasts and led him to give Foster broadcast rights.

By 1935, Hewitt had closed his microphone to everything but hockey. He described his decision in a way that characterized his life. "We don't want to saturate the air," Foster Hewitt said, a modest man that day and to the day his voice stopped altogether, April 21, 1985.

With his lineup sheet spread in front of him in his
broadcast booth high above the Maple Leaf Gardens
ice, Foster Hewitt wove the legends that endured
in the hearts of a nation.

Above and facing page: *The mid-1920s bankruptcy of the Western Hockey League meant the calibre of NHL play became even better, as the stars of the failed league joined team rosters. Brothers Bill (above left) and Fred "Bun" Cook (above right) and Ivan "Ching" Johnson (facing page) were among the WHL refugees who made it big in the NHL. All were a part of the New York Ranger teams that won the Stanley Cup in 1928 and '33. The Cooks, along with Frank Boucher, formed a highscoring forward line that tallied well over 1,000 points in 10 years, while Johnson patrolled the blue line.*

Top left: *In 48 playoff games over his career with the Ottawa Senators and Montreal Maroons, Clint Benedict recorded 15 shutouts and allowed only 87 goals against—a 1.80 average—on the way to four Stanley Cups.* Bottom left: *The dominant NHL goaltender at the turn of the decade was Charlie "Chuck" Gardiner: runner-up for the Vezina Trophy in 1930 and '31, and winning it in 1932 and '34.*

Top right: *An outstanding, versatile goaltender of the early era, Harry "Hap" Holmes won four Stanley Cups with four teams: the 1914 Toronto Blueshirts, the 1917 Seattle Metropolitans, the 1918 Toronto Arenas and the 1925 Victoria Cougars.* Bottom right: *In his first year with the Toronto St. Patricks' starting roster, Cecil "Babe" Dye led the NHL in goals in 1920–21, tallying 35 in 24 games. Twice, in 1922–23 and 1924–25, he was first overall in league scoring.*

In one year, 1928–29, the Canadiens' George Hainsworth (left) accomplished more
than most goalies do their entire career: he notched 22 shutouts, in only 44 games.
When the first Vezina Trophy was awarded in 1927, there was no doubt who the winner
would be, and Hainsworth would sweep the voting the next two years as well. Roy
"Shrimp" Worters (right), at five-foot-two, played far above his size in the nets for 12
seasons with the Pittsburgh Pirates, New York Americans and Montreal Canadiens.
In 1929 he was the first goaltender to win the Hart Trophy, beating out
Irvine "Ace" Bailey, and he added the Vezina in 1931, outshining
the Blackhawks' Charlie Gardiner.

From the depths of the Great Depression came a glimmer of hope. In Toronto, a grand new shrine to the game of hockey, Maple Leaf Gardens, was opened amid pomp and ceremony. Work may have been scarce, and times tough, but as long as the game of hockey was being played, there was the promise of better things to come. As North America's economy ebbed and flowed throughout the decade of the 1930s, so would the fortunes of its professional hockey franchises. In this era of uncertainty arose strong-willed men who bent the future of the National Hockey League upon the anvil of their vision. They took their rightful place in hockey history as builders of the new league. Art Ross in Boston, Major Frederic McLaughlin in Chicago, Jack Adams in Detroit, Léo Dandurand in Montreal, Lester Patrick in New York, Conn Smythe in Toronto—all were autocrats, pure and simple. Yet they were also keen judges of hockey talent. Under their firm direction, the game of hockey changed—for the better—and its players flourished.

Facing page: *Francis "King" Clancy was the heart and soul of the early Maple Leafs. He cost Conn Smythe $35,000—won on a 100-to 1 colt, Rare Jewel—and two players.* Previous pages: *During the Leafs' late-1940s three-straight Stanley Cup run, Garth Boesch and Jim Thomson dive at the Rangers' Buddy O'Connor while Leafs captain Syl Apps and goalie Turk Broda await O'Connor's shot.*

Trainer Tim Daly (left), owner Conn Smythe (centre) and his aide de camp and publicist Frank Selke, Sr. (right) are ready in the early 1930s for the short trip to Union Station, a Pullman car, and points east, south and west.

Red Dutton (left) refined himself over a 10-year career as a hardrock defenceman
with two teams, and then went on to seven years of coaching and management
with the New York Americans, and finally served as president of
the NHL from 1943 to 1946.

Top left: *Nels Stewart was the NHL scoring champion and MVP in his rookie season, 1925–26, and scored the then-phenomenal total of 136 goals and 56 assists over the five-year life of the Maroons' S Line, centring Hooley Smith and Babe Siebert.*
Bottom left: *Alex Connell: the best goalie in a low-scoring era. From 1925–26, when he chalked up 15 shutouts in 36 games for Ottawa, he had 13 in 44 (and a Stanley Cup the next year), and 15 in 44, including a record six straight the year following.*

Top right: *Frank Boucher literally owned the original Lady Byng Trophy after he won it an unequalled seven times in eight years from 1928 to 1935.*
Bottom right: *Hardnosed Albert "Babe" Siebert won the Stanley Cup in his 1925–26 rookie season with the Montreal Maroons and joined the S Line that terrorized the league after 1930. Later on, with the Boston Bruins, he was moved to defence to replace the suspended Eddie Shore, and then became his equally feared partner.*

The 1931–32 season, with Maple Leaf Gardens opened and a new 48-game season, was also a milestone in Jack Adams's engineering of the Detroit franchise. After missing the playoffs four of five seasons, the Detroit Falcons arrived at Montreal's Windsor Station (above) for the second game of their quarterfinal with the Maroons (which they lost). Four years later they would win the Stanley Cup. Star goalie Alex Connell is standing far left with future high scorers Larry Aurie (kneeling, left), Herb Lewis (standing, third from left) and Ebenezer Goodfellow, Hart Trophy winner in 1940 (standing, third from right).
Jack Adams is kneeling, third from right.

Red Horner

All through the 1930s the bad man of hockey was a big-boned, red-headed defenceman for the Toronto Maple Leafs, George Reginald "Red" Horner. For eight straight seasons in a 12-year career he was the National Hockey League's penalty leader and its most punishing bodychecker. Once, unforgettably, he knocked out the rock-ribbed star of the Boston Bruins, Eddie Shore, with a single punch. Right in a raucous Boston Garden, at that.

*Close to royalty in the Toronto of 1932, the Stanley Cup champion Leafs
were popular guests everywhere. During a tour of a local pipe factory,
Red Horner (middle row, fifth from left) and his teammates assumed
the worldly sophistication that a pipe conferred.*

He remembered two hard-nosed stars of the old Montreal Maroons, Nelson "Nels" Stewart and Reginald "Hooley" Smith, testing him in his rookie year. He said, "I had been checking Nels closely. He didn't like it. He and Hooley converged on me. Nels put a two-hander right through my glove, broke my hand. Of course, the equipment back then was primitive."

Red Horner is the sole survivor of a team of Hall of Famers who were his teammates on the nationally heralded Maple Leafs of Foster Hewitt's inspired invention. They seemed nine feet tall, those Maple Leafs, as Hewitt's marvellous voice carried their names from coast to coast: Charlie Conacher, Harvey "Busher" Jackson, "Gentleman" Joe Primeau, Francis "King" Clancy, Clarence "Hap" Day, Harold "Baldy" Cotton, Irvine "Ace" Bailey.

"When I was 19 years of age I was captain of the Marlboro junior hockey club, and I also played in the Broker's League. I had taken a job in the old Standard Stock Exchange in Toronto. One night near Christmas in 1928 I played a junior game on Friday night and I played in the Broker's League on Saturday afternoon. Connie Smythe was at that game, and after the game he came to me and he said, 'Red, you've had enough of this amateur hockey. I want you to come with us.'

"I said, 'That's very nice, Mr. Smythe, when do you want me?' And he said, 'I want you tonight. We're short-handed tonight, and we're playing against the Pittsburgh Yellow Jackets.'

"'Well,' I said, 'thank you very much, Mr. Smythe, but I've only seen one or two pro games in my life, and I don't know your players.'

"'I'll tell you what I'll do,' he said. 'I'll give you $2,500 for the balance of the season.'

"I was only making $25 a week, so the 2,500 looked pretty good to me. I said, 'I'll tell you what I'll do, Mr. Smythe. I haven't got a car; if you'll pick me up on the way to the game tonight I'll introduce you to my parents. If everything works out we'll drive on down to the arena and you can introduce me to the rest of your team.' And that's what he did, and he started me on defence that night with Art Duncan."

Back then, with Horner thumping incoming forwards towards the cheap seats, the team soared in the standings. But curiously, no Stanley Cups followed a relatively easy sweep of the New York Rangers in 1932. From 1933 to 1939, the Leafs were overall leaders twice and division leaders four times. But they drew blanks in five Stanley Cup finals. How come? Red Horner frowned. "There were reasons," he says. He pauses, going back. "Some of our players behaved thoughtlessly. Once we reached the playoffs, you see, they knew they had already earned bonuses. So they didn't take care of their conditioning. They let themselves go just enough that it made the difference by the time we reached the final round."

Horner was on the ice for the Maple Leafs on one of the blackest nights in NHL history. This was the riotous night of December 12, 1933, when Eddie Shore almost killed Ace Bailey. Literally.

"The entire incident took place within a matter of two or three minutes," Red Horner begins. "You must understand that Shore was a terrific player, one of the best defencemen in the league, and that particular night he was on the offensive a good deal. He brought the puck down the ice innumerable times, and we usually checked him at the blue line, King Clancy, my defence partner, or me, and he became irritated by this.

"So this one particular time he came down and I checked him, knocked him out into the corner of the boards. The puck stayed in front of me, and when Clancy took it up the ice, Bailey dropped back into his place. That was our system; when a defencemen took the puck, the wingman on that side came back to his position. In the meantime, Shore picked himself up out of the corner and he charged Bailey from a side angle so that Bailey couldn't see him. I've always felt Shore thought he was charging me because I was the one who was giving him the most trouble. I really believe that.

"At any rate, he charged Bailey from an angle, and Shore was a tremendously strong individual. Shore picked Bailey up like a rag doll and turned him over in the air and Bailey came down on his head. He twisted Bailey in the air, right over his knee. Well, Bailey came down on his head, went into a convulsion, turned blue. I looked at him and I knew there was something seriously wrong. Shore, in the meantime, had skated nonchalantly up the ice and taken his position on the defence. I said to myself, 'He can't get away with this.' And I skated up and I said to him, 'You S.O.B.' and I hung one on his chin. He went down, cut his head on the ice, so there's blood flowing down there on one end of the rink, and there's Ace Bailey out at the other end. It was so serious that you could have heard a pin drop in the arena.

Unfairly fired by the New York Rangers after building their talented first club, Conn Smythe (bottom row, second from right), an engineer by education, vowed to return with a better team. He bought the Toronto St. Patricks' NHL franchise in mid-season 1926–27, changed its name to the Maple Leafs, hired Dick Irvin to coach, kept Hap Day and bought King Clancy from Ottawa, and, on Frank Selke's advice, rebuilt the team with youngsters. Members of the Leafs 1931–32 Stanley Cup-winning team posing at training camp in the fall of 1932: (Top row from left) King Clancy, Ken Doraty, Hal Darragh, Hal Cotton, Joe Primeau, Bob Gracie; (middle row from left) Alex Levinsky, Charlie Conacher, Andy Blair, Red Horner, Ace Bailey, Harvey Jackson, Lorne Chabot; (bottom row from left) Tim Daly, Frank Selke, Hap Day, Conn Smythe, Dick Irvin. Fred Robertson, Earl Miller, Frank Finnigan and Harry Westerby are not pictured.

"The whole Boston team came at me with their sticks up, and our fellahs came out to intervene. Then I believe that everyone thought, 'This is serious,' and they stopped. They saw Bailey's terrible condition.

"Subsequently, Shore was suspended for the balance of the season, and I was suspended for 16 games, a third of the season in the 48-game schedule of the era. We were interviewed by police in Toronto and the essence of the thing was that if Bailey had died, and he was close to dying, Shore would have been charged with manslaughter."

Several weeks later a benefit game was held in Toronto for Bailey, the Maple Leafs against an all-star NHL lineup. "I played in it and so did Shore," Horner remembered. "I was the one who went down to the Union Station and met Shore there, shook hands with him, and took him up to the hotel. We didn't hold a grudge. We never had any trouble. Bailey was in the hospital for five weeks in Boston. He never played again. He had to learn to talk all over again."

Red frequently fought on the ice, but he remembered a newspaper interview with Smythe. "He was quoted, 'When Horner's getting penalties, we're winning games.' That was because when I'd get into scuffles, for one reason and another, I'd usually take another player off with me. So it wouldn't leave the team short-handed. A lot of rookies came into the league during my regime and, me having this terrible reputation, they'd often pick a fight with me so they'd get their name in the paper. I was a clean player. I never hit a player with my stick. I was an aggressive, heavy body-checker. Opposing players didn't like it. But I never started a fight. I was always on the receiving end."

By the mid-1930s Horner began planning for his life after hockey. He took an office job with a prominent coal company in the off-season. When he left hockey following the 1939–40 season he began a slow climb with the company. He became a vice-president and switched to a Canadian firm owned by a Cleveland coal company. When the American owners wanted to sell out, Horner was given first refusal in buying it. He raised the money, bought it, and, at 63 years of age, he sold it for a handsome profit and retired.

Red Horner took a penalty on his first shift in the NHL. In his second game, Christmas night against the Maroons, Nels Stewart broke Horner's hand. Over his dozen NHL seasons, Horner led the league in penalties from 1933 to 1940, set a record for penalty minutes in 1935–36 that stood for 20 years, and was the inspirational leader of the Gashouse Gang Leafs of the 1930s. He became the Leafs' captain in 1938.

Dressed up on his wedding day in top hat and tails,
Clarence "Hap" Day was the first captain of the Leafs, leading them
to their first-ever Stanley Cup (1932) and the first-ever sweep
of a final series. As Leafs coach, he guided them
to five Cups in 10 years.

Top: *Toronto Maple Leafs' fresh-faced "Kid Line." Charlie Conacher (left) was the best player in a family that had members in the NHL nearly every decade since 1925. Joe Primeau (centre) centred the line, setting an NHL assists record with 37 on Toronto's 1932 Stanley Cup-winning team. By 1932, Busher Jackson (right) was the NHL scoring champion, and was voted an All-Star every year but one until 1937. Frank Selke called Jackson the classiest player he had ever seen.*

Bottom: *Teammates on the 1939 and '41 Stanley Cup-winning Bruins were Bill Cowley (left) and Aubrey "Dit" Clapper. Cowley won the 1940–41 scoring title by an 18-point margin, and ultimately, in 1947, would become the NHL's career scoring leader with 547 points, surpassing Syd Howe. In 20 seasons (1927–47) with Boston, Clapper led the Bruins to six first-place finishes and three Cups, and was a six-time All-Star (at right wing and defence).*

Above left: *Fiery Eddie Shore remade the Boston Bruins in his image, an identity that persists to this day. Shore was named NHL MVP four times—more than any other defenceman. After winning his fourth Hart Trophy in 1938, Shore held out that fall and signed for the maximum NHL salary of $7,000.*

Above right: *The NHL's leading scorer in 1928–29 and a Stanley Cup winner in 1932 with Toronto, Ace Bailey was a great penalty-killer and may have been the league's greatest sportsman: He graciously shook hands with the man who nearly killed him, Eddie Shore, at centre ice.*

Above: *The "Stratford Streak," Howie Morenz (seated, far left), the most exciting
player of his time—seen here with the 1916–17 Stratford (Ontario) Midgets—
was voted outstanding hockey player of the first half of the 20th century. NHL
scoring champion three times in his first 10 years with the Canadiens, Morenz
died, legend has it, of heartbreak after a broken leg ended his career in March
1937. His body lay in state in the Montreal Forum, and was viewed by 25,000
fans. Previous page: Syl Apps, Olympic pole-vaulter, captain of McMaster
University's football team, "a Rembrandt on the ice, a Nijinsky at the goalmouth,"
finished 1936–37 second in scoring (by one point to Sweeney Schriner), and won
the Calder Trophy. He made his winger Gordie Drillon top scorer in 1937–38,
again finishing second (by two points). Apps won the Lady Byng in 1942
and led the club to Stanley Cups in 1942, '47 and '48.*

Top: *Howie Morenz at the Ace Bailey Benefit Night, a game between the Maple Leafs and an NHL All-Star team at Maple Leaf Gardens February 14, 1934. More than 15,000 fans donated $20,900 toward Bailey's recovery in "a generous, fine and sporting episode in the sporting city's history,"* the Montreal Herald *reported.*

Bottom: *Aurèle Joliat, a year from retiring after his sparkling 16-season career with the Canadiens, gazes wistfully upon the equipment of Howie Morenz, the Stratford Streak, left on his chair in the dressing room at the Montreal Forum.*

Above: *The Boston Bruins' "Kraut Line" (from left: Bobby Bauer, Milt Schmidt, Woody Dumart) had all played together back home in Kitchener, Ontario, a centre of German-Canadian heritage. The line finished 1-2-3 (Schmidt-Dumart-Bauer) in the 1939–40 scoring race. In 1941, all three took their talents to a higher plane, joining the Royal Canadian Air Force. At war's end, all three resumed their NHL careers with Boston.*

Facing page: *The outstanding Canadian athlete of the first half of the 20th century, Lionel Conacher was only the second-best hockey player in his family, but was a draw in Pittsburgh, New York, Montreal and Chicago, whom he led to a Stanley Cup in 1934. The well-travelled "Big Train" found himself back with the Maroons the following year, and won another Cup with them.*

Part Four

THE ORIGINAL SIX

1945 — 1967

From mid-century, the history of the NHL became a story of titans and dynasties. The survivors of a league that had grown at times to as many as 10 franchises, and had seen teams change names and cities with dizzying regularity in the 1920s and '30s, would settle into an era of stability, known as the age of the "Original Six." The Red Wings, the Blackhawks, the Rangers, the Canadiens, the Bruins, the Leafs: these few teams would symbolize hockey for fans across North America. Early in life, people would form loyalties to one or the other, and hold to them with the same unquestioning fidelity they would, in the same era, bestow upon their religious or political affiliation. The Maple Leafs of the late-1940s and '60s, the Red Wings of the early 1950s, and the Canadiens of the late-1950s and early '60s, would all reign atop the NHL's promontory, and their players — "The Rocket," "The Turk," "Mr. Hockey," "The Golden Jet" — would stride the popular imagination like gods.

Facing page: *Turk Broda was a premier playoff performer with five Toronto Stanley Cup-winning teams.*
Previous pages: *One of the fastest skaters of his day, Bobby Hull would leave opponents in his wake before unleashing his powerful shot.*

Facing page: *Bill Durnan (left), relaxing here with Maurice Richard in 1949–50, was a reluctant addition to the NHL. Enjoying a career in the minors, Durnan didn't welcome the pressure of the big league game. Finally signed by Montreal at age 28, Durnan more than proved his worth, winning the Vezina Trophy an amazing six times in a seven-year career. An innovative player, Durnan wore two catching gloves so he could catch or shoot with either hand. Durnan retired in 1950 claiming his nerves were shot.*

Above: *Maurice "Rocket" Richard (right), the fiery emperor of the Montreal Canadiens dynasty of the 1940s and '50s, was the first NHL player to score 50 goals in 50 games and, eventually, the first to score 500 goals. Harry Lumley (far left) tended goal through 804 regular-season games over 16 seasons with four of the Original Six franchises—the Red Wings, Blackhawks, Maple Leafs and Bruins. In 1953–54, playing for the Leafs, he led the league with a rock-bottom goals-against average of 1.86.*

Top: *Fan favourite Leonard "Red" Kelly was part of the Red Wing defence that registered four shutouts in eight straight victories to win the 1952 Stanley Cup. He won three more Cups with Detroit before being traded to Toronto—where four more Cup victories awaited.* Bottom: *A record-breaking goal-scorer as a junior, George Armstrong signs his first Leafs contract in 1950, accompanied by his mother, Alice, while Conn Smythe (far left) looks on, and Hap Day offers a steadying hand. He went on to spend 20 seasons in the NHL, 12 as the Leafs' captain.*

Facing page: *Andy Bathgate blew out his left knee on his first shift with Guelph in 1949–50. After a complete recovery, he and the Mad Hatters won the Memorial Cup in 1952. Although he joined the New York Rangers for the 1952–53 season, Bathgate really hit his stride in 1958–50, when he scored 40 goals and won the Hart Trophy. In the 1961–62 season, he was made captain and responded by equalling Bobby Hull's points total, but lost out to Hull for the Ross Trophy because he had scored fewer goals.*

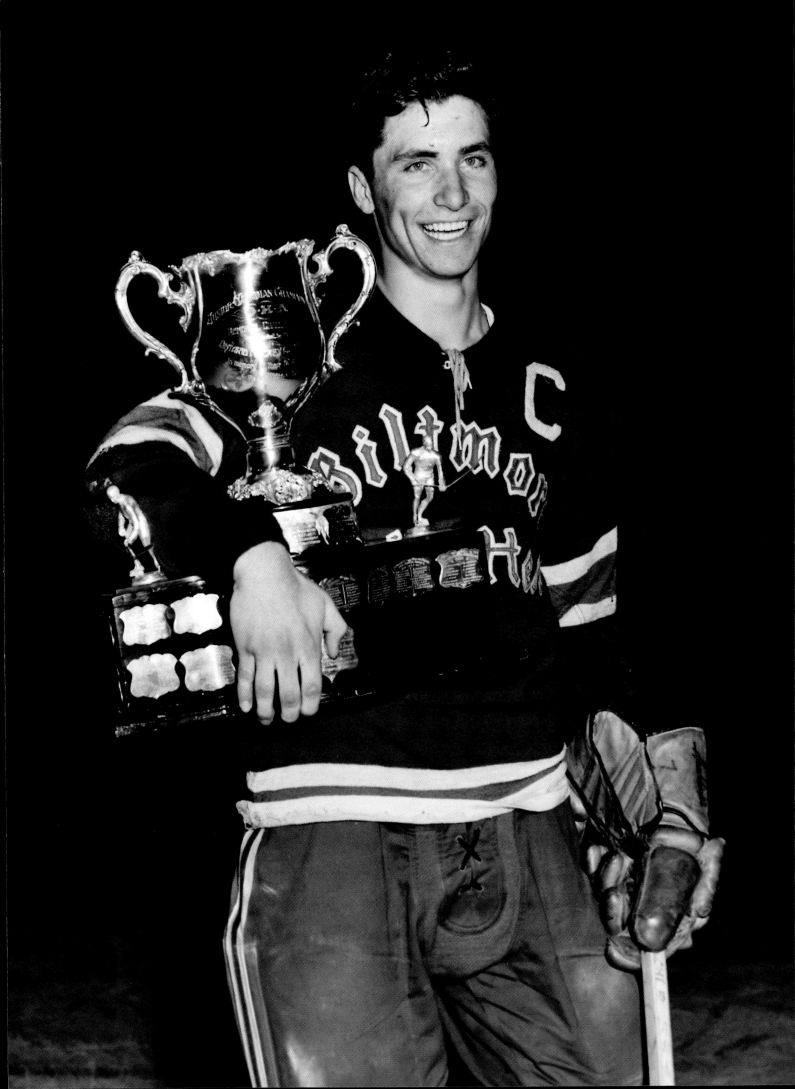

Teeder Kennedy

Soon after Theodore Samuel "Teeder" Kennedy's mother gave him his first pair of skates he developed a burning ambition. He wanted to be "another Charlie Conacher." He was only seven years old when Dan Chambers, who owned the Port Colborne dairy, took him to Toronto to see the first two games of the 1932 Stanley Cup playoffs. Ted had been fascinated by the sight of Conacher firing those rocket-shots from the right wing. Conacher wore the number 9 jersey.

Emulating his hero, Kennedy insisted on wearing the number 9 jersey through his minor hockey career.

However, when he became a Maple Leaf on March 7, 1943, Lorne Carr was wearing number 9. Kennedy was issued with the number 20 for the last two games of the 1942–43 season, and later when Syl Apps was away at war he wore number 10, Apps's number. When Carr retired after the playoffs of 1946, the Maple Leafs decided that Kennedy finally should have the opportunity to wear number 9. At the next season's opening game, Charlie Conacher made a special on-ice appearance to present his old number to the beaming youngster.

The Kennedys lived only a block from the Port Colborne Arena where his mother operated the concession stand. This gave the boy the opportunity to be the quintessential rink rat. When he was playing pre-teen hockey, some of his teammates had difficulty pronouncing "Theodore." Quickly the name was truncated to Teeder and it stuck with him after a *Welland Tribune* reporter described him as Teeder Kennedy in the newspaper.

When he moved up to play junior hockey for the Port Colborne Sailors, Kennedy had the good fortune to be coached by Nels "Old Poison" Stewart, who had been one of the NHL's brightest offensive stars when he played for the Montreal Maroons, Boston Bruins and New York Americans.

"Stewart was a great teacher," Kennedy says now, "Always, he had been a magician around the other team's net. He taught me the technique of being smart around the goal. He was an excellent role model. I was fortunate to be in the right hands."

Kennedy was only 17 when he joined the Toronto Maple Leafs in March 1943. The Leafs had obtained the rights to Kennedy from the Montreal Canadiens in exchange for the rights to young defenceman Frank Eddolls. Ted was in Port Colborne in March 1943 when Nels Stewart called him from Toronto. Stewart said that Frank Selke and coach Hap Day of the Leafs wanted to talk with him. Stewart told Ted to hop on the afternoon train and he'd meet him at Toronto's Union Station. That evening, he signed a contract with the Maple Leafs.

He'll never forget his first sight of the Maple Leafs' dressing room. He rode a street car from his boarding

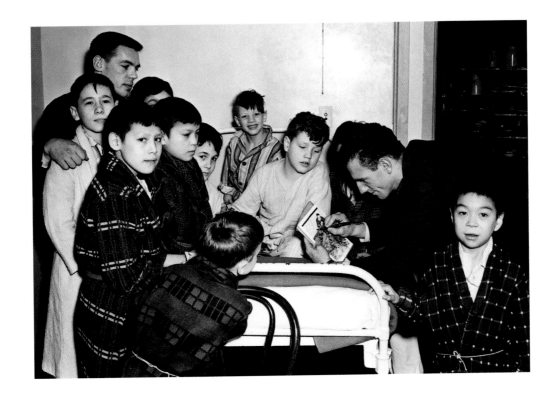

Top: *Hockey heroes, present and future Leaf
captains, autograph programs for sick kids.
The youngest-ever Leafs captain, Kennedy (right),
and Howie Meeker (far left), quietly represented
the team on and off the ice.*

Bottom: *If any single picture could sum up
Ted Kennedy's well-rounded life, this image of
postwar domestic bliss is it. Teeder relaxes at
home with his wife, Doreen, and their
Doberman pinscher, Max.*

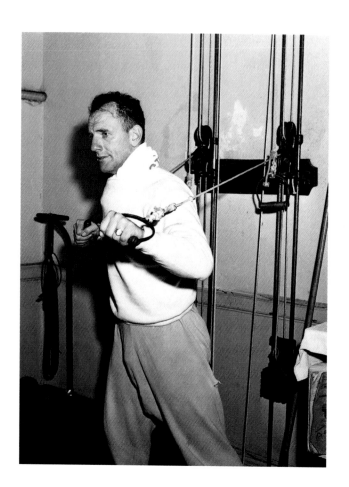

Although not a great skater, Ted Kennedy's hard work and dedication helped to make him one of the best face-off men of this time. Sid Smith, also a Leafs captain, attributed Kennedy's success to the fact that he had "more gumption" than most.

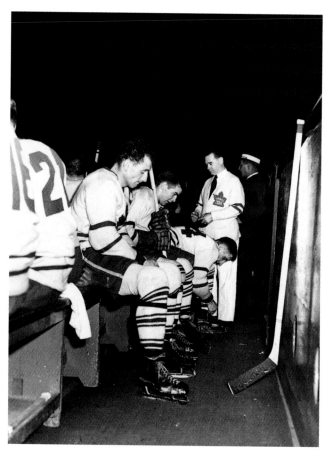

The captain catches his breath after a shift during the Leafs' dismissal of Boston in the 1951 semifinal that led to their sensational five-game, all-overtime Stanley Cup victory over Montreal. Both Kennedy and Maurice Richard scored sudden-death markers in the series.

house to the Gardens. He walked into the dressing room and was given a seat between Sweeney Schriner and Billy Taylor. The room was in uproar—Babe Pratt was shouting insults at the grumpy old trainer, Tim Daly. Finally, Daly pulled a large knife and threatened to use it on Pratt. Kennedy was alarmed, but he learned that these Pratt–Daly shouting matches were daily performances that kept the players amused.

Kennedy had arrived wearing a new parka, which he thought was quite nifty. But Pratt whisked him out of the Gardens later; steered him downtown and made him buy a regular overcoat so that "you'll look like a Maple Leaf."

The Leafs were down to their final three games of the schedule when Kennedy arrived. He played in two of those games—both on the road against Boston and New York. The Leafs didn't dress him for the playoffs. So, a home crowd didn't see him perform as a Leaf until the opening home game of the 1943–44 season. He made an instant hit, scoring the first goal of his NHL career.

The Maple Leafs weren't destined for glory in that season; the Canadiens bounced them out of the first round of the playoffs. However, Kennedy had a tremendous rookie season, with 26 goals and 23 assists.

What he describes as "the most memorable victory of my career" was just around the corner. The Maple Leafs won the Stanley Cup in the spring of 1945, defeating Detroit in an amazing seven-game series, featured by the goaltending of Toronto's Frank McCool and Detroit's Harry Lumley. The Leafs won the first three games and the Red Wings won the next three. Toronto won the final game in Detroit, 2-to-1, when the irrepressible Babe Pratt jammed a goal-mouth pass into Lumley's net.

Kennedy would play on five Toronto teams that won the Stanley Cup and he won an honour that eluded his hero, Charlie Conacher. In 1955, Kennedy was awarded the Hart Trophy when he was adjudged to be the NHL player most valuable to his team.

Looking back over the years, Kennedy remembers Hap Day as "absolutely the best coach—and I'm not forgetting Dick Irvin, Toe Blake and Punch Imlach. Hap was the complete analyst. He made a close study of every opposing player, and his pre-game instructions to us always were from the defensive standpoint."

He remembers the players of his days with great admiration. He recalls Billy Mosienko and Doug

Bentley of the Blackhawks as the "greatest skaters." He remembers Gordie Howe as "the greatest all rounder." In summation, he says: "All things considered, I'd have to name my teammate Syl Apps as the perfect centreman. The goalies who gave me the most trouble were the Big Men—Bill Durnan and Chuck Rayner. To appreciate the greatness of Rayner, you must remember that he played on some very weak New York teams."

Hockey historians seldom permit Ted Kennedy to forget the night of Tuesday, March 28, 1950, in Detroit when the Leafs and the Red Wings met in the first game of the Stanley Cup semifinals. The Leafs were leading, 3–0, when Kennedy carried the puck out of the Toronto zone, along his left wing boards. He saw Gordie Howe coming towards him on collision-course. At the last split second, Kennedy braked —Howe crashed head first into the dasher, atop the boards.

Gordie's skull was fractured. He was rushed to hospital and for days he lay unconscious, on the critical list. Eventually, he made a complete recovery. The following season, he played the full 70-game schedule and led the NHL in scoring. Although Red Wings general manager Jack Adams provoked the Detroit media into sensationalism by alleging that Kennedy was responsible for the injury, Ted says simply: "Gordie and I never made body contact. He went right past me, into the boards."

Ted Kennedy, raised in the old Ontario work ethic, was keenly aware that hockey wasn't the only thing in life. For several years before he retired from the NHL in 1957, he spent the off-seasons working for Canadian Building Materials, owned by Larkin Maloney, who was Conn Smythe's horse-racing partner. It was an appropriate business connection. Ted had been interested in horses since childhood when Dan Chambers, the Port Colborne dairyman who took him to his first NHL game in 1932, gave him an old thoroughbred named Rob Roy.

Today, he's back living in Port Colborne—only a quarter-mile from his boyhood home. There, he is nourished by the memories of his devoted mother, his mentors—Nels Stewart and Dan Chambers— and an old horse named Rob Roy.

For a man with the near-military bearing of a Teeder

Kennedy, the opportunity to shake hands with

the future queen was the highlight of a lifetime.

As captain of the 1951 Stanley Cup champion

Maple Leafs, Kennedy was the ideal

representative for his country.

Red Storey

Past or present, few people have been
in a better position to observe the release of
passions that hockey provides than R. A. "Red" Storey.
Red was the on-ice official in the Montreal Forum
the night berserk fans ignited what became known
as the Rocket Richard Riot. Later, officiating
a playoff game in Chicago, in the din of garbage and
noise directed at him, a fan charged onto the ice
and splashed a bucket of beer in his face.

"There's often a funny side to something like that," Red recalls, laughing. "I was ready to drop the puck when the Chicago centre Tod Sloan said to me, 'Red, if you'd known that guy was gonna throw beer in your face, would you have opened your mouth?'"

Red and a brother and three sisters were raised by their mother: "My mother did everything. She did the laundry, she did people's cleaning, she did neighbours' chores—anything at all to survive.

"My sister Irene was a world-class sprinter. There was a field across from our house where I took a hand lawn-mower to clear a 100-yard track for her. She made the Olympic team, but she was told at the bank where she worked if she took time off to go to the Olympics she was fired. So she stayed home."

In the early 1940s, Red was living in Montreal and working at Canadian Car and Foundry. He played senior lacrosse with the local Shamrocks and senior hockey with the local Royals. In lacrosse he still holds a Quebec record: 12 goals in one game. When Hockey-Hall-of-Fame builder Robert LeBel founded the Quebec Interprovincial Senior hockey league in 1944, he asked Red if he would like to referee.

"The funny thing is, I never knew anything about the rules of any game—I just played," Red says. "When Bob LeBel asked me to referee I said 'I don't know anything about the rules.' He said, 'I didn't ask you that; I asked you if you'd like to referee.' I said sure. And that's how I started out officiating hockey."

He soon learned the rules, of course, and in time, through common sense and experience as a former player he became a top referee. But looking back he does not find his nine-year NHL career the most difficult period of his life as an official.

"This may sound strange to people on the outside, but the toughest hockey I ever refereed was junior hockey. You got guys with hair-trigger tempers all hell-bent to make it to the pros and show everybody up and run around like horses just let out in the field. You've got to be on your toes to control situations like that.

"I worked in the Quebec senior league and it was tough to get out of some of those places. I remember working at Quebec City where the cops had to pull their guns to get us off the ice. A guy named Kenny Mullins and I were working the Quebec Aces and the Sherbrooke Saints when the crowd came on the ice after us. Both teams formed a circle to keep them away from us and they got us to the room. We both

It was customary for a new referee to take on the linesman's role for his first tour
of duty in the NHL, as Red Storey (left) did in 1953. Here, wearing the white
officials' sweater of the early 1950s, he warms the bench with referee
Hugh McLean (centre) and linesman Sam Babcock.

Storey lays down the law to team captain Ferny Flaman and his Boston
Bruin colleagues, as Hall of Fame member George Hayes (centre) looks on.
The striped shirts, adopted in 1950 after a period of fluctuating
fashions for officials, led to them being called zebras—"not the
worst thing I've been called," Storey has said.

showered and we're standing there nude, drying off, and I looked at a brick wall and the wall is coming in. I mean, a brick wall is coming in.

"I yelled to Kenny, 'Kenny look what the hell's happening here,' and we both picked up a chair, and Mullins said, 'That first son of a bitch is gonna be in for a surprise.' Anyway, as the wall came down a door opened up from the other side and the cops came in with their guns out. And we're in the middle, and nude. Hey, that was a sight. That woulda shook 'em." Red guffaws.

Another scary time was the night of the Richard riot in Montreal. What led to it was a decision by the league president Clarence Campbell to suspend the idolized Richard late in a season of violent outbursts. In Boston Richard had swung his stick above his head with both hands like an axman and struck a Boston player, Hal Laycoe, across the shoulder and head. Richard broke free from restraining linesmen to strike Laycoe again and then he punched a linesman, Cliff Thompson.

Following an investigation, Campbell read his decision: "Richard will be suspended from all games, both league and playoff, for the balance of the current season."

The city's fans were stunned, then wrathful. Anonymous callers pledged to kill the league president. Two nights later Detroit went into the Forum tied with the Canadiens for first place. Campbell sat in his box through the first period while fans booed, hissed and threw eggs and assorted debris at him. A smoke bomb exploded nearby. People began to cough and rub their eyes. Fearing a panic, the city fire director ordered the Forum evacuated. A further uproar followed the P.A. announcement that the game had been forfeited to Detroit. Campbell was led from the building through a side door.

"When I woke up that morning," Red recalled, "I turned on the radio and the disc jockey was saying, 'Is this March 17th, St. Patrick's Day, or is it Blow-Up-the-Sun-Life-Building Day?' That's where the NHL offices were.

"And when I went down that evening there were a few more people circling the Forum, but I figured that's okay, it's a big game tonight. A few minutes before we're going on the ice a guy came in and says, 'Geez, it's really getting bad out there. The people have to put their coats over their heads to get in the building now. They're throwing bottles at the building and glass is falling all over the people.' And that was before the game. The game finished at nine o'clock and I didn't get out the back door until one-thirty the next morning. It was terrifying."

The 1959 playoff in Chicago wasn't that bad, but it was bad enough. The old Chicago Stadium was unique. "In a building supposed to hold 16,000 they'd cram in 20,000," he recalls. "Even before they started the game they had to clean up the garbage. They'd turn out the lights, put the spotlight on the flag for the national anthem and when the lights were out everybody'd throw garbage at the referee."

This night, following two instances when Red didn't call penalties, fans went on the ice. One threw beer, another was axed by Doug Harvey. There was blood on the ice, deafening noise and a minute and a half to play, Montreal leading by 5–4, when Red called for NHL president Campbell. "He was in charge of the series. I wanted to find out if he wanted the game called off, or if he wanted to continue, but he wouldn't come and see me. I asked him later why, and he said he feared for his safety."

The blood on the ice stopped people from coming over the boards, but the old stadium remained an angry cauldron. Finally, Red was able to get the teams organized to play and they completed the final minute and a half. Then he headed out, as he remembered, for a couple of brews to replace his lost liquid from the sweat of stress. "The first bar I went into, a guy says, 'There was a guy here with a gun; he's gonna shoot you.' It was some night."

The next night he was in Boston for a semi-final game between the Bruins and the Maple Leafs. He got a message to go to Campbell's hotel room. The president told him to pay no attention to newspaper statements attributed to him.

"Now, we go over to Jack Sharkey's bar and the kid comes through with the papers and I buy every one he's got," Red recalls. "And it's headlines. I'm talking three-inch headlines. 'Storey Chokes: Campbell,' 'Storey Chicken: Campbell.' I read the papers and I turned to Eddie Powers, my backup referee, and I said, 'Eddie, go get a night's sleep. You're refereeing tomorrow.' Eddie says, 'Don't be crazy, Red.' And I said, 'Eddie, I'll never work for that man again as long as I live.' And I never did. I resigned."

Throughout a career that included refereeing more than 2,000 hockey games, Storey's bravery was never called into question. Red Storey explains to Ted Lindsay (right) and Toronto's Harry Lumley (left) his reversal of what at first appeared to be a Detroit goal.

Jean Béliveau

Many prospects come into the National Hockey League with expectations of greatness, but no player's arrival in the NHL was so widely anticipated as that of Jean Béliveau. When he first attended Montreal's training camp as a 19-year-old, he was unofficially anointed the next star of the Canadiens, heir to Rocket Richard. For four seasons, through his play in junior and senior leagues in Quebec City, a team, a city, a province and the hockey world awaited the rangy centreman's debut.

Top: *In one of his last games with the Quebec Aces, Jean Béliveau sweeps around Wally Clune of the Montreal Royals. Béliveau was the scoring champion both years he played for the Quebec Aces of the Quebec Senior Hockey League, where he was coached by future Toronto Maple Leafs coach Punch Imlach.*

Bottom: *A flabbergasted Béliveau is presented with a 1951 Nash Canadian Statesman de Luxe after his junior Quebec Citadels beat a Montreal Junior Canadiens team loaded with Charlie Hodge, Dickie Moore and Scotty Bowman in their Quebec playoff. Béliveau was expecting "a nice watch and a couple of well-wishing speeches."*

Of the heroes of his youth, Béliveau says, "I remember very clearly listening to the radio when Maurice Richard scored 50 goals in 50 games. The next morning, on that little ice surface while we were playing our shinny games, we were 'broadcasting' the game. One player was Maurice and another one—usually me, because I've always played centre—was Elmer Lach. I've always felt that Maurice showed us that, if you really desire something, if you really work at it, it's possible for any young Quebecer to make a career in hockey.

"I went to Montreal's training camp every fall and people always asked me when I was going to join the Canadiens," Béliveau says. "My father advised me not to sign the C form, the contract that would tie me to the team. I know that I could have played for Montreal when I went to that first training camp. In the end I know that it was best for me as a hockey player and a person to stay in Quebec."

In Quebec, shrewd hockey men were charged with overseeing his development on the ice, among them Roland Mercier, manager of the junior Citadels, and George "Punch" Imlach, coach of the senior Aces. "If I had gone to the Canadiens maybe my progress would have been different," Béliveau says. "I wouldn't have had so much ice time as I did with the Citadels and the Aces. The Quebec senior league was very high quality. Lots of players had NHL experience. And Punch Imlach helped me a great deal. He told me to be successful I was going to have to work on getting a quicker first step. He was right. After practice he worked with me and even had players chasing me to get that better first step."

Béliveau joined the Canadiens for the 1953–54 season and was a far more polished player than the teenager whom Montreal general manager Frank Selke had desperately tried to sign for three seasons. His numbers, 13 goals in 44 games, were solid if not sensational. By his third year he made his imprint on an emerging dynasty. In 70 games in the 1955–56 campaign Béliveau racked up 47 goals and 88 points, both league-leading totals, and he won his first Hart Trophy. In the playoffs he again showed the way, accelerating the pace with 12 goals and 19 points in 10 contests against the Rangers and the Red Wings. It would be the first of Montreal's five consecutive Stanley Cup championships.

"The 1955–56 season was my best hockey," Béliveau says, "but overall the teams in '57 and '58

In one of their many classic confrontations in an all-time great rivalry,
Terry Sawchuk drops from his trademark crouch position to cover the short
side as Béliveau charges for the net. A leader both on and off the ice, the
name Jean Béliveau is synonymous with the skill and grace that typified
the great Montreal teams of the 1950s and '60s.

were stronger. By then Henri Richard had joined the team, and that gave us two strong scoring lines with Maurice Richard, Boom Boom Geoffrion, Dickie Moore, Bert Olmstead, Henri and myself, and a great defensive line with Phil Goyette, Donnie Marshall and Claude Provost, who became famous for shutting down Bobby Hull with Chicago. Defensively, there was Jacques Plante, the greatest of his era, in goal and Doug Harvey and Tom Johnson on the blue line. It was a team without weakness."

Not only did this team lack weakness, it also possessed an enormous strength in character, and much of that emanated from Béliveau. "When I came to the Montreal training camps from Quebec and when I first joined the team Butch Bouchard and Doug Harvey taught me a lot about leadership," Béliveau says.

It is a mark of Béliveau's personality that what he describes as "one of my greatest joys of my career" came not from heroics and triumph on the ice but rather from respect and recognition from his peers, when he was named team captain in 1961. "It came as a shock to me, a complete surprise," he says. "I was not even an alternate captain. Everybody put a slip of paper into Toe's hat and he counted the votes. I almost fell off the bench when he announced that I was the new captain. Tommy Johnson, Dickie Moore and Boom Boom were the alternates. It was such an honour. Later I realized that it was my temperament, my way of doing things, that won me the support of my teammates, and I realized that I had different expectations to live up to."

The Canadiens' championship teams of the 1960s have not been so highly regarded as the Montreal squads that imperiously won five straight Cups in the 1950s. Yet Béliveau believes that the later-vintage Habs were close if not equal to the storied team that featured Rocket Richard, Doug Harvey and Jacques Plante. "We won four Stanley Cups in five seasons, only losing to Toronto in '67," says Béliveau.

"We had a bunch of Hall of Famers and a lot of guys who were very underrated. With Yvan Cournoyer, who was on the wing on my line, and Henri Richard, we probably had the two fastest skaters in the league. Two other guys, Gilles Tremblay, another of my wingers, and Bobby Rousseau were only a step behind them. On defence Jacques Laperrière, Terry Harper and Ted Harris were tougher than anybody to get by and J.-C. Tremblay handled the puck better than anybody."

Perhaps the most dramatic moment in his estimable career was reserved for his last season, Montreal's run to the Cup in 1971. "In 1970 we missed the playoffs and I intended to retire," Béliveau says. "I came back only because our general manager, Sam Pollock, asked me to play one more season and help out with a team that had a lot of young players. In the first round of the playoffs we faced Boston, the best team in the league. Phil Esposito and Bobby Orr led the league in scoring that year. But I felt that we had a chance whenever we put on the Canadiens' sweater, and I told my teammates that.

"We lost Game 1 in Boston 3–1, but Game 2 turned the series around. We were down 5–1 in the second period and 5–2 at the start of the third. I scored two goals in the third period to get us to within one. Then Jacques Lemaire, John Ferguson and Frank Mahovlich scored. We won the game 7–5, and it was a new series. We won that series in seven and, after beating Minnesota in the next round, we beat Chicago, winning at Chicago Stadium in Game 7 on a long slapshot by Lemaire that beat Tony Esposito."

Though he led the Canadiens in scoring during his last regular season, Béliveau entertained no thoughts about coming back. "Maybe I was a little sad that I couldn't end my career with a game in the Forum," Béliveau says. "But on the plane ride home from Chicago I remember talking with Fergie about it. I was 41 and I didn't have much more to give. Fergie told me that he was going to retire too, that Réjean Houle had been carrying him for a couple of months. I knew then that playing our last game at home was not so important as knowing when our time has passed."

Béliveau's retirement marked the passing of an era. In his 1,125 NHL games, Jean Béliveau scored 507 goals during the regular season and was an integral part of teams that won 10 Stanley Cup championships. No one could ever have expected that a young man from Victoriaville would have handled the attendant celebrity with such grace and dignity. The Canadiens' greatest captain will forever be remembered and respected for his classy manner more than for any goal or Cup victory.

"My father worked for the power company in Victoriaville and he knew nothing, really, about hockey," Béliveau says. "But he taught me so much about life. He told me, 'Be honest. Always give your best and do a little bit extra.'"

Teammates in victory. The stellar Montreal
Canadiens squads that celebrated five Stanley
Cups in seven seasons from 1964–65 through
1970–71—interrupted only by Toronto in 1967
and Boston in 1970—included immortals such
as (left to right) Henri Richard, Jean Béliveau,
John Ferguson and Yvan Cournoyer.

Bill Mosienko rode the right wing on the Blackhawks' famed Pony Line of the
1940s. His linemates, brothers Doug and Max Bentley, won the NHL scoring
title three times between them. Here, Mosienko shows off the three pucks he used
to score the fastest hat trick in NHL history—three goals in a record 21 seconds
of the third period against New York's Lorne Anderson on March 23, 1952.
Gus Bodnar assisted on all three, setting a record himself.

Chuck Rayner (right) played his entire 10-season NHL career with New York City teams: the New York (later Brooklyn) Americans and the Rangers. He shares a post-game victory moment with Neil Colville (centre) and Phil Watson (left). Following page: In his first five NHL seasons, Terry Sawchuk, seen here as a fresh-faced teenager, may have been the best goalie ever, backstopping the Wings to three Stanley Cups during that period. The much-travelled Sawchuk played for five NHL teams and received Rookie-of-the-Year honours in three professional leagues. Sadly, his career was cut short by his accidental death in 1970.

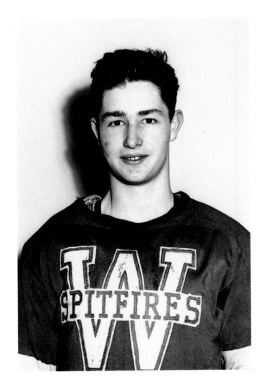

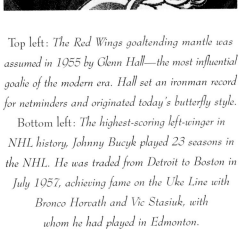

Top left: *The Red Wings goaltending mantle was assumed in 1955 by Glenn Hall—the most influential goalie of the modern era. Hall set an ironman record for netminders and originated today's butterfly style.*
Bottom left: *The highest-scoring left-winger in NHL history, Johnny Bucyk played 23 seasons in the NHL. He was traded from Detroit to Boston in July 1957, achieving fame on the Uke Line with Bronco Horvath and Vic Stasiuk, with whom he had played in Edmonton.*

Top right: *A young Pierre Pilote looked forward to a quietly impressive NHL career with the Blackhawks. He finished second to perennial Norris Trophy winner Doug Harvey in 1962, then swept the trophy three straight years.*
Bottom right: *Alex Delvecchio played a large part in three Stanley Cups with the Red Wings, then settled into the role of respected elder statesman, winning three Lady Byng trophies over the balance of his 24-year career.*

Facing page: *With an NHL career that spanned 21 seasons, Gump Worsley was always at the top of his game, playing on four Montreal Stanley Cup-winning teams during the late-1960s. In 1952, Bill Gadsby (far left) was flying high as the 25-year-old captain of the Chicago Blackhawks. Then a bout of polio stopped him short. Miraculously, Gadsby recovered well enough to be selected to the first All-Star team three times with the New York Rangers.*

Above: *A teammate of George Armstrong's on the Copper Cliff Redmen junior team, Tim Horton's puck handling skills made him a key member of the Leafs when he joined the team in 1952. From 1961–62 through 1966–67, Horton and the Leafs won the Cup four times, and three times Horton made the first All-Star team. Here Horton is pulled down in front of Blackhawks netminder Harry Lumley.*

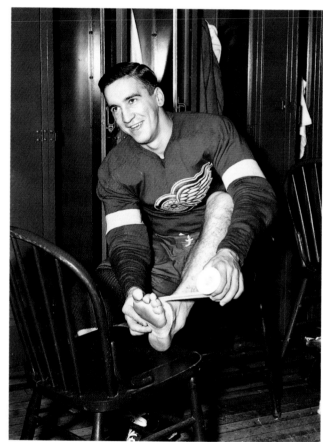

Above left: *Stan Mikita rivaled his more flamboyant teammate, Bobby Hull, in offensive prowess. Mikita, two-time Hart Trophy winner, four-time NHL leading scorer, and an All-Star every year from 1962 to 1970, planes the tool of his trade, one of the first curved sticks in the league, which he is credited with inventing.*

Above right: *Ted Lindsay, one of the best all-round left-wingers ever to play, dressed for 1,068 games over 17 seasons. Known for his toughness, "Terrible Ted" played on four Detroit Stanley Cup-winners, was the top scorer in 1950, and was second (to linemate Gordie Howe) three times.*

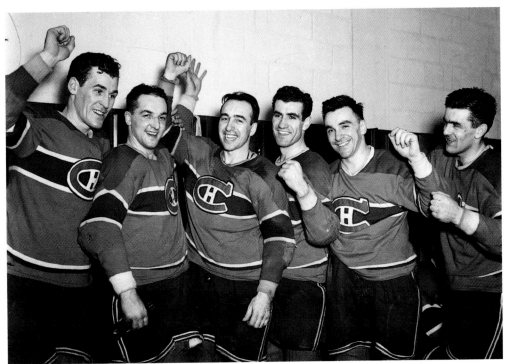

Top: *Ab McDonald, Ralph Backstrom and Bernie "Boom Boom" Geoffrion celebrate another Stanley Cup victory. Montreal teams dominated the league in the 1950s, winning an unequaled five straight Stanley Cups. Geoffrion, often credited with originating the slapshot, was the first player to equal Maurice Richard's seemingly unattainable 50-goal season record, nearly 16 years to the day after the Rocket set the mark.*

Bottom: *Hall of Famers Emile Bouchard (far left), Toe Blake (third from left) and Maurice Richard (far right) with teammates in the Habs' locker room. Richard's early years with the Canadiens brought quick success. Stanley Cup victories in 1944—the club's first since 1931—and in '46 bracketed this photograph, taken on March 24, 1945. That season, 1944–45, Elmer Lach, Richard and Blake finished 1-2-3 in scoring, but the Canadiens fell to the Leafs in the Cup semi-final.*

Gordie Howe

$\mathcal{I}$f the road of Gordie Howe's life had mileposts, there'd be skates and elbow pads hanging on it—the skates to mark the turnoffs, the pads as warning signs for those who faced his all but matchless skills. The first skates dropped out of a gunnysack, shaken on a linoleum floor in the Depression years in Saskatoon. "A lady had come to the house looking for a little money to get her family some food," Howe recalls.

Gordie Howe's 1941–42 bantam team, the King George Athletic Club of Saskatoon, for which he played defence. Howe, at 14 (back row third from right), stands beside Mrs. Frances Hodges, whose family maintained the outdoor rink on which he played around the clock.

"My mother went to the cookie jar where we kept what little we had, and gave her some. A little while later the lady returned and handed mother the sack—saying thank you, I guess, giving back what she could. When mother turned it over, a pair of skates fell out.

"I grabbed one, my sister got the other, and out we went to where the water had frozen over on the garden. When Edna got cold and went in and took the skate off, I grabbed it. Now I had a pair. Now I could actually skate. She never saw those skates again."

Skating began on the garden by day and continued by night along the ruts left by passing traffic. "Back then they never scraped the roads, so the ruts would fill and freeze," he says. "They were like our own special roads, and we skated all over the city."

But small boys grow, and where do you find the money for skates when there's barely money for food? "We were on relief," Howe says. "And what that meant was they gave you shoes—thick ones, like construction boots—and when they wore out you took them down and turned them in and they gave you another pair. But my dad convinced them one time to let me keep the old ones, because all he had to do was punch some holes in the soles, screw in a pair of those old steel blades, and there were my new skates."

A brand new pair of Red Horner blades were earned in exchange for farm work. "If loving something means you never take your skates off, then I was in love with the game. My mother used to put papers on the floor so I could walk in, eat my meals and get back out there."

Today, what he and his friends got up to would draw shudders. Back then, it was adventure.

"We'd skate on the Hudson's Bay Slough. Sometimes the ice would be rubbery, and when the water filled in behind your stride you kept moving or you'd fall through. In a way, that's how I got into organized hockey: because one day we heard a scream behind us, and Frank Sheddon had fallen through."

Sheddon was supposed to go to peewee tryouts "but by the time we got him home he was so cold and stiff he looked like a sheet on a clothesline." So Sheddon's father gave Gordie his son's skates—"nickel-plated, the most beautiful things I'd ever seen. Just wearing them made me faster"—and the Detroit organization had itself a budding legend.

Top: *Detroit trainer Lefty Wilson surveys the damage from an Eddie Shack high stick in January 1961. Although Howe received a concussion and a 12-stitch gash to the forehead, his legendary toughness had him back in the lineup after missing only three games.*

Bottom: *A great player at both ends of the ice, Howe could be relied on to help out the defence as well as score goals. Here Howe knocks down a centring pass in the Red Wing zone against Toronto in front of goalie Terry Sawchuk. Doug Barkley covers the Leafs' Bert Olmstead.*

Because he was small and a bit scrawny, he began school hockey as a goalie—another break, in that it taught him to shoot with both hands. "I caught with the left, which made the right one the top hand on the stick," he explains. "In order to shoot the puck or the tennis ball I'd have to shoot it left-handed. It just became automatic. I didn't even realize it until Jack Adams stopped me at Detroit's training camp one time. 'Do you do that all the time?' he asked. 'Do what?' I replied. 'Change hands,' he said. 'I dunno,' I said. It had become so natural I'd never noticed."

But it was as a winger, not as a goalie, that he went to the Wings' camp, a big, rough-edged 17-year-old whose shoulders were beginning to show the promise of what was to come. His number was 9 almost from the start—not because he liked it ("I was happy with the 17 they gave me at first.") but because low-numbered jerseys meant you got the lower berth on the team's train trips.

He came in to camp truculent, and fought everything that moved, because he figured that was his ticket to stay. Jack Adams straightened him out. "Young man," he said. "You cannot score from the penalty box. I will not ask you to run from a fight, but please do not go looking for it."

"Thank God," Howe says now. "Where would I be today if he hadn't. I'd never have lasted. I would have been fighting anyone. He taught me to be aggressive, but controlled. Mind you, I liked being the protector. It's different now, they assign people to do that. When I was out there, I just took care of it. I mellowed a bit as I got older, but when I was playing in the WHA against the Russians and one of them hurt [my son] Mark I went out and played against the guy who did it. When I came out of the corner, he didn't."

The gentler, mellower Howe has become the game's elder statesman, the man against whom all others are measured. His seasons covered better than a quarter-century, and perhaps the names and the scores might fade. But his memories of childhood heroes and the responsibilities they engender today are crystal clear.

"Heroes? I was in every garbage can in Saskatoon looking for the Beehive corn syrup labels, because when you collected so many you could send them in and get a picture of a player. I had 180 pictures and there were only 120 players in the league, because when you wrote in and asked for one guy they sent you another if they didn't have him ready. So I'd wind up with a bunch of Syl Apps and Turk Broda cards, which was great because I could trade them.

"But my big hero was Ab Welsh, who my Dad knew. He took me right into the dressing room to get autographs. Then he looked at me, asked me which way I shot, and came out with a stick.

"I slept with that thing! God, I never had such a gift. But on the way home I thought to myself, 'I've missed a very important part of hockey: signing autographs. I'm going to have to do that some day.'

"So I went home and took the autographs I had and tried to copy some of the ways the names were written. I came up with some Gordie Howe signatures and got to the one you see today."

Years later, that signature is still in demand and never denied, although sometimes the slow-but-wicked Howe humour comes through. Standing in the lobby of the Bayshore Hotel in Vancouver a few years ago he was approached by two elderly ladies who timidly asked if they could please have his autograph.

"Absolutely not," he snapped.

Then, as they stood there, stunned, he flashed the Howe smile and cocked his finger like a pistol.

"Gotcha!" he said, and spent the next 10 minutes talking with them as he signed.

Gordie Howe's place in the record book is secure. Only Wayne Gretzky, the 10-year-old he befriended at a banquet and years later played beside in a WHA All-Star game, has more goals and points. It doesn't matter, for Howe is beyond numbers.

How, then, would he like to be remembered?

"I guess, probably, the word would be respect," he says. "Respect gave you more room, and if you get a little more room to manoeuvre then you're going to be a better hockey player.

"I played a little rough. I shaded the rules a little bit. I remember against the Russians somebody was bugging Wayne. 'Just flush him down the right side,' I said, 'and when you hear me, get out of the way. I'm going over the top of him and teach him a lesson.' And I did.

"That's the way I played the game: not to get revenge, but to get respect. It would make me very happy to be remembered with respect."

Although he won both the Art Ross and the Hart
Trophies four times, Gordie Howe's achievements
transcend awards. He played major-league hockey
with two of his sons; was loyal to a single team for
a quarter century; scored his 1,000th goal with a
broken shooting hand and played top-flight hockey
well into his 50s—the very fabric from
which legends are made.

Johnny Bower

Goaltenders live in their own worlds. They are allowed to hang around with hockey players but they aren't really hockey players. They just stand there, not actually playing hockey but playing punching bag or pin cushion or dart board, always on the receiving end, seldom permitted to go out and belt some guy back. Playing without a mask all those years, Johnny Bower figures he took 250 stitches in his face alone. Then there were the usual sprains and muscle pulls and hand injuries.

But for him the facial bumps and bruises were the most frequent. "You get hit over the eye, it swells. There'd be a lump. They'd put a leech on," he says.

It seems the club trainer kept a leech in a solution on the infirmary shelf, and he'd take it out with a pair of tweezers and place it next to the lump. The leech would edge over, examine the lump, then clamp onto it and have a meal. "The leech would get fatter and fatter and then, pop, down he'd go and the swelling around the cut would go, too."

"I used to get broken fingers," Bower says of the big shooters—Hull, Howe, Bernie "Boom Boom" Geoffrion, the Montreal right-winger who invented the slapshot. "Hull was tough, but I honestly think Bobby's brother Dennis had a harder shot. Bobby was accurate, he'd aim for the corners and you could get set for him, but Dennis had a rising shot, like Frank Mahovlich, a wild shot that Dennis didn't know where it was going and neither did I."

"That Rocket," Bower remarks, remembering the Habs' great captain. "I could never figure him out. He'd never shoot to the same spot. He'd be low, high, the stick side, the glove side. Jacques Plante used to tell me how the Rocket practiced and practiced in Montreal, forehand and backhand. Jacques said the Rocket could close his eyes and pick any corner he wanted. The guy used to drive me nuts."

"And Gordie Howe," Bower smiles, thinking back. "He'd had a quick sort of half-slapper. He'd wait and wait for the goalie to move first, then he'd let go. Snap!"

Johnny Bower, close to a quarter-century in professional cages, cannot remember when he didn't want to be a goaltender in the National Hockey League.

"When I was a little kid in Prince Albert, Saskatchewan, where I grew up, I'd listen to Foster Hewitt. My hero was Frankie Brimsek and my team was the Boston Bruins because they had Brimsek. He was called Mr. Zero. I wanted to be like him.

"We had a big family. I had eight sisters and a brother. My father worked in a packing plant in P.A. He didn't want me to play hockey. He thought hockey was too rough, that I was getting hurt a lot. I played junior for the Prince Albert Mintos. We played Saskatoon one playoff when they had Gordie Howe and

Key performers in both the 1963 and '64 Toronto Maple Leafs–Detroit Red Wings finals, Gordie Howe and
Johnny Bower show mutual respect during an interview with Frank Selke, Jr. after Game 7 of the 1964 final series,
Toronto's third consecutive Stanley Cup victory. Although Bower would retire in 1970 after a 25-year career,
Howe would remain in the game until 1980, a phenomenal 35 years in professional hockey.

After eight seasons with the Cleveland Barons of the American Hockey League and an impressive rookie season with the Rangers in 1953–54 (70 games, 2.60 goals-against, five shutouts), Bower seemed destined for immediate stardom. But Gump Worsley's return to New York and the realities of a six-team league sent Bower back to the AHL for three more MVP seasons. It was not until Punch Imlach drafted Bower in 1958 that he found his rightful home: the Toronto net he tended for the next 12 seasons. Here, Bower clears the puck past teammates Ivan Irwin and Danny Lewicki, and the Leafs' Jim Morrison and Joe Klukay.

Vic Lynn, who later was with me on the Leafs. They beat us. I worked, too, a railroader. I was a boiler-maker's helper. I cooled off engines, made sure their wheels were good.

"A scout for Cleveland, named Hub Wilson, saw me play and that's how I got to be a pro. He sent me to St. Thomas, Ontario, where the Cleveland Barons trained. They were in the American Hockey League, which was a real good league at a time when the National League had only six teams. My first year was the 1945–46 season, the first of eight years in Cleveland."

The Barons were always a contender and frequently the league champion, but as the years slipped past Bower grew frustrated that he was still a minor leaguer. Then he'd remind himself that there were only six NHL teams. "I was right behind the six best goaltenders in the world and I kept trying to improve."

The Barons sent him to Detroit to see Terry Sawchuk play. "I wrote down everything: the way his stance was, the way he crouched, how he played the angles. He came out to challenge shooters very slowly, he glided out. I wrote down how he cleared shots to the corners with his stick.

"I used to be a flopper, down a lot. Maybe that's why I stayed there so long, in Cleveland.

"Anyway, when I came back I told our coach, Bunny Cook, 'I've got to work on my angles.' Bun, who had played on the famous line with his brother, Bill, and Frank Boucher, said okay, and he'd stay out and shoot pucks at me. He had a tremendous shot, Bunny did, even at his age. He'd watch me very, very close and he told me right off the bat, 'Look, you're coming out too fast. Slow down, *slow down*.' I was coming out to challenge far too fast, off balance, my whole body and my stick was off the ice. The other way, the way Sawchuk was, he would glide out with his stick on the ice watching the shooter all the time. I realized I had to smarten up."

Finally, Bower was recognized. The New York Rangers made a deal for him in 1953. Soon after his arrival the regular goaltender, Charlie Rayner, drew him aside. "He said to me, 'Look, I've been watching you, and you've got problems handling the puck. You skate around too much.' See, I'd stickhandle with it; he'd fire it to somebody, head-manning it.

"It was with the Rangers that I started poke-checking guys cutting in. That was my baby, sliding out on my stomach with the stick flat out, right at the knob at full extension. That way, if you miss the puck you get the guy between the legs, tripping him—accidentally, of course."

But in that first NHL exposure with the Rangers, Bower still wasn't a fixture. He played the full 70-game schedule and had a gaudy 2.60 goals-against average, but in the fall one day after practice in 1954 the coach, Phil Watson, called him aside. Bower well remembers the conversation.

"'Here's your ticket,' he told me. 'You're going to Vancouver. Work hard and you've got a chance to make it up here.'"

And he did fine. But in the autumn of 1955, Lorne "Gump" Worsley, five years younger, retained the Ranger job and Bower was dispatched to the Providence Reds, where he played for two more seasons. Then the Rangers sent him back to his old stomping ground, Cleveland. There, he was seen in excellent form by the coach of the Springfield Indians, one George "Punch" Imlach. So, in 1958 when Imlach became the boss in Toronto he drafted the veteran he remembered in the Cleveland cage.

"Punch had faith," Bower says. "I admired him. One time in the playoffs he opened a bag in the dressing room and threw down piles of money, 100s and 20s and 50s, thousands of dollars. Pointing to the money, he told us, 'That's how much each guy gets if you win the Cup.'" Bower laughs. "We won it, too," he says.

Punch knew when Bower was through. He sent him to an eye specialist who told him that the concentration over the years of peering at a little black disk had taken its toll. He bought glasses. Then one night in St. Louis in 1969 a young defenceman, Noel Picard, scored his only goal of the season, a long shot on Bower. "A shot from the blue line," Bower says, a trifle sheepishly. "A hard shot, low by my right foot. I missed it. I told Punch, 'I was screened.'"

"'Screened,' he cried. 'There was nobody in front of you!'"

And so Johnny Bower sat down in his 25th year in professional hockey. "I'd accomplished something I'd wanted since I was a small boy," he says. "To play in the National Hockey League. And my greatest thrill was going into the Hockey Hall of Fame in 1976, because it was an achievement, wasn't it?"

Johnny Bower, the ageless one, shares a moment
with his son Johnny Bower, Jr. during the Leafs'
March 1960 semifinal playoff series with Detroit.
Even though it meant a life filled with bumps and
bruises, Bower always wanted to be a goaltender.
In a time when being the seventh-best netminder
in the world led to a career in the minors,
Bower continually worked to perfect his craft.
The effort paid off in spades as Bower fulfilled his
life-long dream with a 25-year professional hockey
career and election to the Hockey Hall of Fame.

Bobby Hull

66 "We had an old Philco radio," Bobby Hull recalls. "About 49 knobs on it, and none of them did anything but turn it on or off or change the station. My Dad didn't believe in antennas, so it never had a piece of wire on it or anything that might help bring the stations in. So I'd listen to Foster Hewitt doing the Leafs games on Saturday nights, and he'd fade in and out like he was in a wind tunnel."

Bobby Hull was an attraction—as much for opponents as for the millions
who idolized him. Here, Leafs defencemen Allan Stanley (second from left)
and Tim Horton combine to slow his progress toward Terry Sawchuk
in the Toronto net, while Red Kelly moves to scoop the puck.
In the top left-hand corner is none other than Phil Esposito,
the future "Slot Machine."

But he listened, the small boy who would someday be the "Golden Jet," the first man to do what had always been deemed impossible: break the 50-goals-in-a-season record of the immortal Rocket Richard; the man who led the hockey revolution by jumping to the upstart World Hockey Association with the Winnipeg Jets, giving it the vital credibility jump-start and changing the game forever. He listened so hard and so often that even today he can do the play-by-play.

"It was Thompson to Mortson to Kennedy to Meeker to Lynn. And Syl Apps and Bill Barilko and the guy from Winnipeg Foster loved to call, Wally Stanowski.

"'He's behind the Leaf net! He's at the blue line! He's at the red line! He's at the blue line! He's in the corner!' I don't think Wally Stanowski ever got in front of the net. Not to hear Foster, anyway.

"There were all those guys and so many others on the other teams—the Howes, the Lindsays, the Abels—but it was always 'Kennedy to Meeker to Lynn—Chicago's got the puck. He shoots, he scores!' No one ever seemed to have the puck except Toronto until the other team scored."

A child of the pre-television generation, he would sit and listen to the radio, visualizing his heroes streaking up and down the ice. But the mental pictures came nowhere near the reality. "When I went to Maple Leaf Gardens in 1949 and saw how big the building was, and how colourful, and how ballerina-like the players were," he says, "it was unbelievable."

He was given his first pair of skates the Christmas before his fourth birthday, venturing out onto the ice between his two older sisters. Family legend has it that before the day was over he was skating and they were having trouble catching him. "Possibly a little far-fetched," he concedes, "but I know I couldn't ever wait for winter to come. I'd have my stuff on two or three times in the summer, just checking it out and pretending. And there was never any doubt that I'd be a professional hockey player. It was a question of me getting old enough or big enough, and then it would happen."

It happened, but Hull's route to the Chicago Blackhawks and the glory years that followed was almost derailed before it started. He was, in fact, going to be in the Detroit Red Wings chain, and had a letter to that effect written by the legendary Tommy Ivan on Detroit stationery.

He was playing bantam hockey for Belleville in the second game of a total-goal playoff against Peterborough. Things were not going well. "The kid who got to play goal for us in the first game was there because he was the son of some city official, and he couldn't stop a beach ball. They beat us by six goals on our home ice. That was my first scuffle with authority. I told the coach we either got someone else in goal for the second game or I wasn't playing.

"'Who do you want in goal?' the coach asked. Well, we had this little guy forward, Abby Wright, no bigger than a minute, but quick and strong. 'Put Abby in,' I said. 'He'll do better than that other guy.' So he did, and we go to Peterborough, and beat them by five. We were one goal shy of a shot at playing in Maple Leaf Gardens!

"I think I got three goals and an assist or something like that. Detroit had a scout in the stands, a man named Red Creighton. He told them about me, and there I was, getting ready to go to Windsor and play for their junior club, the Spitfires, and go to Assumption College. But in those days, NHL teams who sponsored junior teams automatically got the rights to all players within a few hundred miles of the town. When the Blackhawks found out the Red Wings were scouting someone in their territory, they wrote to the Wings and told them in no uncertain terms that this Hull kid was their property and had been on their list since he was 13. My dad kept that letter for so long it must have fallen apart from folding and unfolding it, because I've never found it in his effects."

He has no specific recollection of walking into the Chicago dressing room that first time, perhaps because he was staring at the faces of the people dressing around him—Lindsay, Eddie Litzenberger, Glenn Hall, Nick Mickoski, Gus Mortson...

"It was different then," he says. "Six teams, 120 players, you knew everyone. There were no names on the back of the jerseys, but that didn't matter. I didn't even need numbers. I knew them all by the way they skated. It was a more personable game. The fans knew us all. They'd wait outside to say hello or rub shoulders with us. When we went into an opposing building the people were seeing individuals they had come to know and adore or dislike. We were flesh and blood. Now people who watch from up above have

*Bobby Hull's game was speed and firepower. Hull could skate at 30 mph
and shoot at close to 120, reinforcing his "Golden Jet" nickname.
He was propelled by a spectacular physique that he built pitching
hay on his father's farm at Point Anne, Ontario.*

no idea what players look like without their helmets and masks unless they happen to see them in ads.

"It's a funny thing about the helmets. We survived without them, but when they put them on, players lost respect for each other. Because the helmets were there, nobody worried about keeping the sticks down. Now they were head high and players started getting cut, and it became a poorer game for it."

Asked to name his most memorable game, he hedges at three. Three games, three different meanings.

"The night I broke Richard's and Bernie Geoffrion's record and got the 51st goal, not for the record but for the ovation the Chicago fans gave me. They wouldn't quit. They stomped and they whistled and they hooted and hollered—they just wouldn't quit. They were showing me how they felt about me, and it was special.

"The game I played a few days after Bruce MacGregor accidentally swung his stick and broke my nose and the orbital rim of my eye and severed the sinuses with two-inch cuts up my nose. I scored three goals and had an assist and they beat us 6–4, but to be able to come back after such a severe injury and compete against the Howes and Delvecchios and Ullmans and still be able to perform at a high level meant a lot to me.

"Third, and maybe number one, the night I finally got to represent Canada in 1974 in Quebec City against the Russians. Standing there on the blue line listening to the anthems, it seemed to me that I was being raised off the ice by some unknown force. I know this: On the first shift the puck came up the right side, a perfect pass to me, and I could not put my stick down on the ice to take the pass! It was a feeling I'd never had before, and never did again."

He is one of the game's legends now, and frank enough to admit it and acknowledge the responsibilities that go with it. "It's good for the country, good for the world, to have people who young folk can look up to. It's even better when they're the stature of the guys I played with—pretty well every one of them good heads, good hearts, good people. Kids need heroes and they need dreams. Who knows—some day they might be the ones coming through the dressing room door and signing scraps of paper.

"If their own heroes have been the right ones they'll remember what it was like, and never be in too big a hurry to stop and say hello."

Bobby Jr. and five-year-old Brett Hull hold Dad's three-puck 500-goal plaque the night of February 21, 1970, after Hull's 861st game, in Chicago vs. the Rangers. Bobby Hull was the third player after Maurice Richard and Gordie Howe to hit this milestone, and he accomplished it in fewer games than anyone until Phil Esposito in 1974, with 803 games. After 658 games, Brett Hull is heading into the 1996–97 season just 15 goals shy of that marker, and looks set to achieve it faster than anyone other than Wayne Gretzky.

A triumvirate of Hall of Famers: With Jean Ratelle checking him from behind, the speedy Henri Richard protects the puck from an Ed Giacomin poke-check in a game during the 1965–66 season. Richard's speed and agility made him a familiar sight to the goalies of the six-team league. He put together an achievement that may remain unmatched. In 20 seasons with the Canadiens, between 1955–56 and 1974–75, he won 11 Stanley Cups. Inheriting Elmer Lach's sweater number 16 following Lach's retirement, Richard actually tallied more total points than his older brother, Maurice: 1,046 to 965. Jean Ratelle centred the "GAG (Goal A Game) Line" for the Rangers between wingers Vic Hadfield and Rod Gilbert. In 1967–68, Ratelle and Gilbert placed fourth and fifth in league scoring, behind only Stan Mikita, Phil Esposito and Gordie Howe. For a decade from the mid-1960s to the mid-'70s, Ed Giacomin was a standout between the pipes at Madison Square Garden. In 1971, he and back-up Gilles Villemure won the Vezina Trophy. His contributions were recognized by a grateful Rangers team when his jersey number— number 1—was retired.

Above: *In a classic goal-mouth confrontation,
Toronto captain George Armstrong (far left) snaps
the puck past Montreal netminder Jacques Plante
and beats him on his glove side, adding yet another
page to the story of one of sport's greatest rivalries.
In 1959 Plante stood alone as the only goaltender
to wear a protective mask—he perfected and
introduced the goalie mask to the NHL.*

Facing page: *Sharing in victory, Frank Mahovlich
holds the Stanley Cup alongside Toronto trainer
Tommy Naylor after the 1967 finals, one of four
opportunities he would get to drink from the Cup
with the Leafs. Mahovlich would again share in
Cup victory in 1971 and '73, playing with his
younger brother Peter in Montreal.*

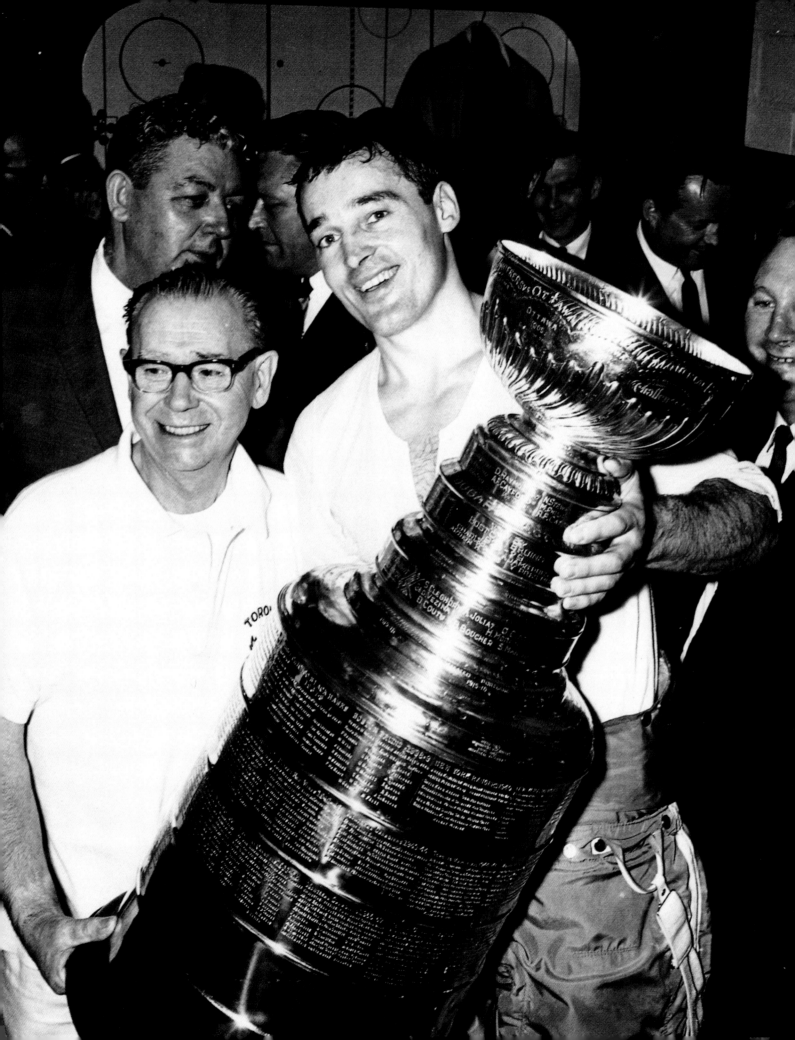

Part Five

THE MODERN ERA

1967 — 1996

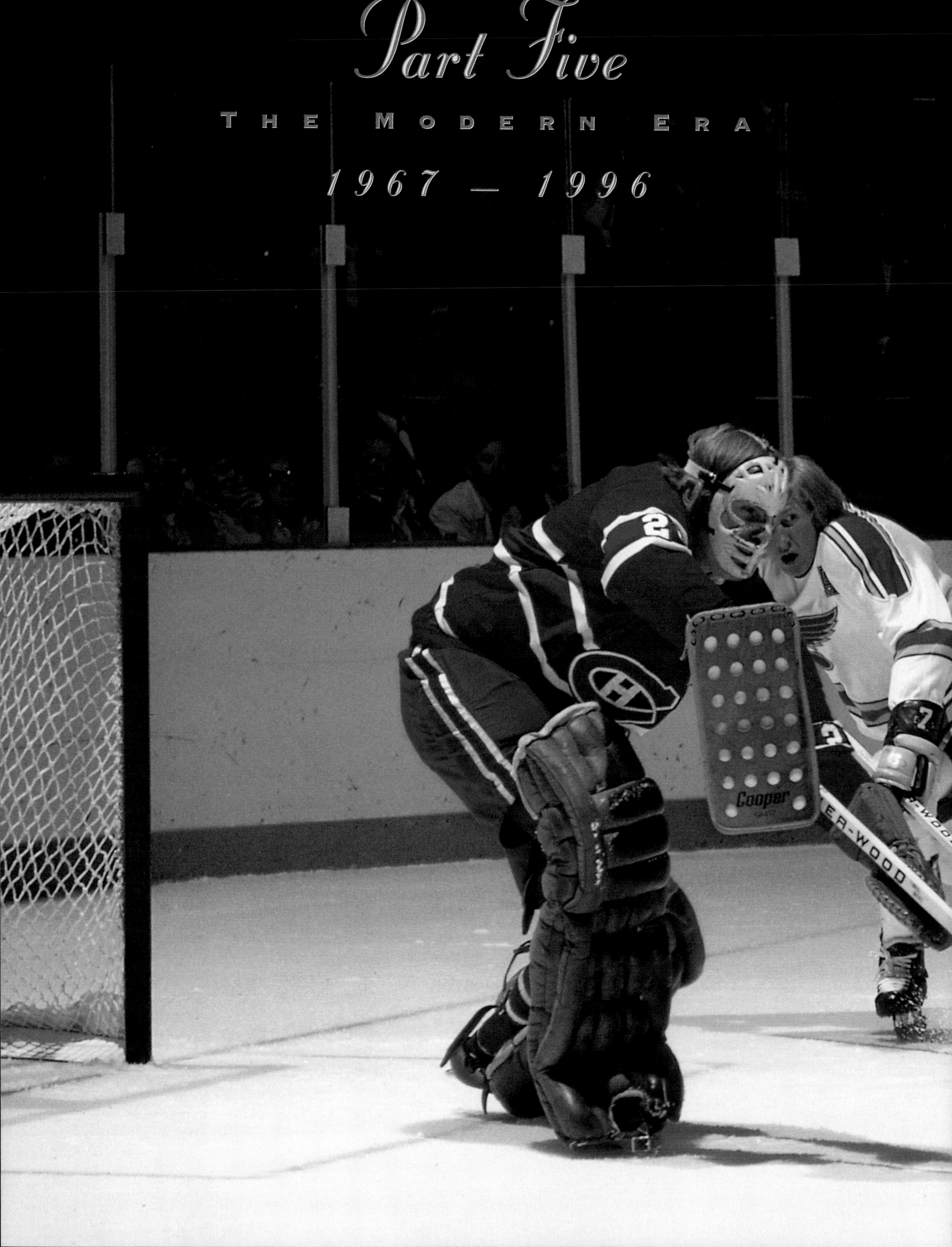

When the days of the "Original Six" ended in 1967 and the National Hockey League doubled in size, a simpler era came to a close. Some complained that growth meant dilution, that the quality of play would never be the same. Yet their fears would come to nothing. Expansion brought opportunity to many talented players who might have been victims of the numbers game in the old six-team league. The size of the NHL would more than double again before the end of the millennium—with new franchises awarded, and some teams absorbed from the rival World Hockey Association. Expansion would bring hockey to more communities across the land, where new legends could grow. The horizons of North American hockey would expand, too, to encompass the world. From the "Summit Series" against the Soviet Union, to the "Miracle on Ice" at Lake Placid, and beyond, as European players joined the rosters of NHL teams, a metamorphosis would take place. As it had at its origin, so once again, the National Hockey League could boast it possessed the best hockey players in the world.

Facing page: *Bobby Orr, a teenage phenomenon, broke the Ontario Hockey Association scoring record for defencemen at age 15, when he starred with the Oshawa Generals. Previous pages: Ken Dryden's legendary goaltending skills gave his Montreal teammates the confidence required to excel at their own game. Here, Serge Savard looks on as Bob Murdoch checks Phil Roberto while Garry Unger makes for the net.*

Facing page: *It is often said that Bobby Orr redefined how the defensive position was played, but his imitators have yet to match the superlative standard he set over 12 seasons with Boston and Chicago. He won the Norris Trophy as the league's best defenceman an incredible eight straight years, from 1908 through 1975. Above: Gerry Cheevers was the Bruins' great money goalie. After winning two Cups in three years, he left for Cleveland of the World Hockey Association. Cheevers's trademark mask bore the marks of stitches he would have needed without it.*

Above: *Phil Esposito, often set up by Orr, became a goal-scoring machine for Boston, winning five scoring championships in the eight years he played for the Bruins, and although he began his career with the Blackhawks in 1963 and ended it with the Rangers in 1981, it is as a Boston Bruin that Phil Esposito is best remembered.*

Facing page: *Tony Esposito, known as "Tony O" to Blackhawks' fans for his propensity for blanking the opposition, tallied 76 shutouts in 886 career games. He won three Vezina Trophies and was a key to Canada's victory in the 1972 Canada-Soviet Union Summit Series. His 1971–72 goals-against average of 1.77 has not been beaten since.*

Brad Park

Veteran players believe that a rookie should "know his place" when he arrives at his first National Hockey League camp. Back at his first training camp with the New York Rangers in 1968, Brad Park knew his place, though probably not in the fashion that the old guard had imagined. "When I came to camp that first season, the Rangers had a veteran blue line," Park says. "They had Harry Howell, who had won the Norris Trophy.

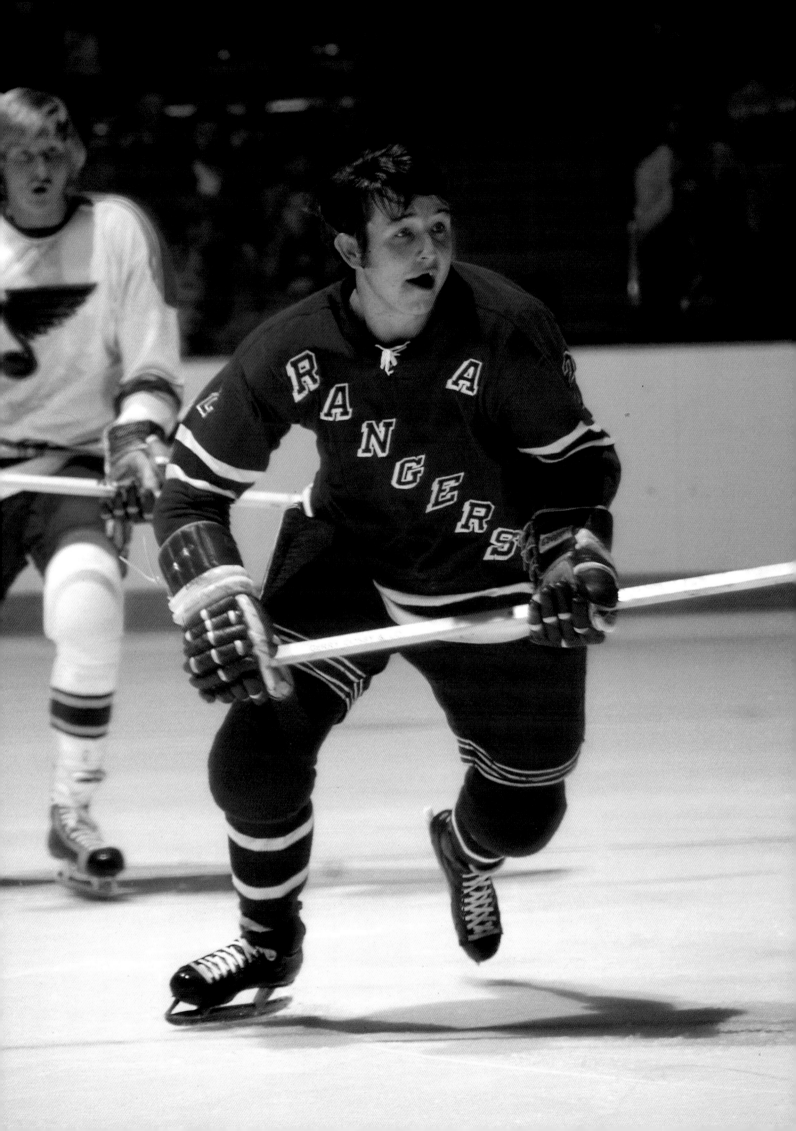

Brad Park, a product of the Toronto Marlboros talent pipeline, arrived in the NHL
one year after Bobby Orr. Brimming with confidence at his first pro training camp,
Park cracked a formidable blue line corps of veterans and All-Stars
to join the Rangers' defence.

They had Jim Neilson, who had made an All-Star team, and Rod Seiling and Arnie Brown, established veterans. But I had a great training camp right from the start. A week into camp a bunch of New York reporters came up to me and asked if I thought I had a shot at the number 5 spot on the Rangers' defence. I told them, 'Actually I'm looking at the number 3 job.'"

This would have been brash talk from a rookie, forgettable stuff, if he hadn't been able to back it up with his play. Brad Park more than backed it up. "Just from a week at camp I knew I could play at this level," he says. "I skated as well as the other guys, shot just as hard, hit just as hard. The only thing they did better than me was thinking on the ice. They thought faster, recognized situations faster and better. I knew that I'd have to work at that."

If Park needed to think more clearly on the ice, he proved astute off it. Before his first training camp, he and his father negotiated his first contract with the Rangers' general manager Emile "The Cat" Francis. Although he received only the NHL minimum salary, Park signed a contract contingent on one special request. "My father and I told The Cat that I'd sign if I was paired up with Harry Howell," Park says. "I knew that I could learn a lot by watching Harry, but Harry really went out of his way to work with me."

Park proved to be a quick study. After his second season with the Rangers, he was voted to the NHL's 1969–70 first All-Star team. In the next eight campaigns, he was elected to the first All-Star team three more times and to the second All-Star team twice. Although he never won the Norris Trophy, he finished second in the balloting six times: four times runner-up to Boston's Bobby Orr, twice to the New York Islanders' Denis Potvin. Park played some of his best hockey for the most stirring series of his era: With Orr sidelined with injury, Park and partner Gary Bergman were the only defencemen to play in all eight games of the Canada-Soviet Union Summit Series of 1972. And Park logged more ice time than any other skater on the team.

Short years before his first training camp with the Rangers, all of this seemed a long way off. At age 15, Park was a highly skilled left-winger in minor hockey in the Toronto suburb of Scarborough. "I had been on skates since age three and I had a pretty good understanding of the game passed on to me from my father," Park says. "He came to Canada from Scotland when he was about five and, though he never played organized hockey, he understood the game and coached the teams I played for from peewee to midget. At home he showed me how to play two-on-ones and three-on-twos on the kitchen table using salt and pepper shakers and ketchup bottles."

Still, at 15, Park was only five feet tall. "It wasn't until I had a growth spurt at 16, when I shot up to five-foot-eight, that I could even think about going somewhere with hockey. That was the year I moved back to the blue line."

Park's study of the Rangers' Harry Howell was only the advanced stage of his apprenticeship. Park first went to school on the blue line of the Toronto Marlboros. "I started analyzing players, really breaking down how they did their jobs," Park says. "The three players I watched the most were Tim Horton, who was incredibly strong but knew how to beat players with just a little deke or feint, Bobby Baun, who was a ferocious body-checker, and J.-C. Tremblay, an absolute magician with the puck. Playing with the Marlies at the Maple Leaf Gardens, I got to see a lot of Horton and Baun and got to see the other teams practice."

By the time Park made the NHL, he was borrowing liberally from the games of Horton, Baun and Tremblay and adding his own touches. More than any of these players he possessed a cannon from the point, a slapshot that rivaled Bobby Orr's. And from his first days with the Blueshirts, he was the team policeman.

The Rangers had been perennial also-rans prior to Park's arrival. Subsequently, the team moved into the league's elite, in no small part due to the presence of Park. New York was one of the league's most exciting teams during the early 1970s but could not bring the Stanley Cup back to Broadway.

"We had a great line-up with the GAG line of Rod Gilbert, Jean Ratelle and Vic Hadfield, as well as Walter Tkaczuk and Bill Fairbairn on the second line and Ed Giacomin in goal," Park says. "The heartbreak was intense, getting close but not winning in those seasons. Still, you have to remember that these were great teams that won the Cup. We lost to the Bruins in six games in the '72 final when Boston had Orr and Phil Esposito playing their best hockey. The one team that knocked us out that I believe we were

Brad Park lines up for a faceoff opposite Yvan Cournoyer. Park was a smooth puck
handler with an uncanny ability to move the puck up the ice. His smooth skating
and powerful shot made him a force at both ends of the ice.

better than was Philadelphia. The Flyers knocked us out in the semis in '74, but that year, Bernie Parent was as hot as any goaltender has ever been."

After that disappointment against Philadelphia, team captain Vic Hadfield was traded and the Rangers named Park as his successor. "That was the highest compliment that I was ever paid," he says. "I was just 24 and became the youngest captain in the franchise's history."

After a loss to the Islanders in the first round of the 1975 playoffs, time seemed to be passing the Rangers by, and the team was ripe for changes. Still, nobody in hockey expected an overhaul like that undertaken by New York management early in the 1975–76 season, nothing less than the biggest trade in hockey history: Park, Jean Ratelle and Joe Zanussi to Boston for Phil Esposito and Carol Vadnais. "We were on the road at our hotel when I got the news," Park says. "It was emotionally very hard because I was a guy who bled Ranger blue and Boston, well, the Bruins were our arch-rivals."

With the trade came the prospect of a blue line pairing for the ages: Park and Orr. Sadly, because of chronic injuries to the latter, this dream defence and, for opponents, power-play nightmare, was short-lived. "Don Cherry was the coach then," Park says. "His plan was that Bobby and I wouldn't play together in even-strength situations, but one of us would be on the ice at all times, controlling play, and we'd both be on with the power play. We lost the first game with that set up but won nine in a row after. The power-play was magic while it lasted. Both of us could handle the puck and shoot it. It seemed like we were scoring at about 50 percent on the power play for that stretch of games. But after those games, Bobby's knees got so bad he couldn't go anymore."

Park finished his career with Detroit in 1985. In 17 seasons, he won honours and accolades but never a Stanley Cup. "That was a disappointment," Park says. "But the Stanley Cup has a lot to do with being in the right place at the right time, nothing you have control over. The first priority of any player is just to make the league and to do well."

At his first training camp Brad Park knew he'd make the league and do well. But not even the most presumptuous rookie could have known that his place would one day be the Hockey Hall of Fame.

Six times, Brad Park was runner-up for the
Norris Trophy. A great defenceman in the era
of great defenceman, it was only the names Orr
and Potvin that separated Park from recognition
as the league's premier rearguard. In a 17-year
career, Park was a standout on defence for
both the Rangers and the Bruins.

Although an outstanding junior player, Bobby Clarke (left), a diabetic, was considered an unlikely candidate for NHL stardom. He spent 15 years proving everyone wrong as he led the Flyers to redefine hockey in the 1970s, winning two Stanley Cups. Twice capturing the NHL scoring title, Clarke was a leader with the Canadian team in the fabled 1972 Summit Series. Here Clarke races Henri Richard to the Flyers' blue line during the early 1970s.

Top left: *Gilbert Perreault was poetry in motion. Bobby Orr admired the way he offered the puck, but never lost it. Perreault passed his idol Jean Béliveau's goal-scoring total before retiring after 17 seasons in the NHL.* Bottom left: *A joy to watch for 18 seasons, Rod Gilbert was the greatest New York Ranger of the modern era. When he retired in 1978, he was second only to Gordie Howe in lifetime regular-season points as a right-winger.*

Top right: *Ed Giacomin was a spectacular and acrobatic attraction in the Rangers' nets for 10 seasons and won the 1971 Vezina Trophy* Bottom right: *Vladislav Tretiak was a shock to North American hockey in 1972 as he stunned the NHL's premier players with his goaltending prowess during the epic Canada-Soviet series. An international star of the first magnitude, he is the only Russian-born player to have been inducted into the Hall of Fame.*

A great Leafs captain, and one of the best players to hold that post, Darryl Sittler was perhaps the prototypical Canadian hockey player—hard work, dedication and perseverance being the hallmarks of his 13-year career in the NHL. On February 7, 1976, in a game against the Boston Bruins at Maple Leaf Gardens, Sittler scored six goals and four assists to set an NHL single-game points record that still stands.

The Montreal Forum, the site of his first NHL goal, provided the location for a
storybook ending to Lanny McDonald's illustrious career: He scored the winning
goal to bring the Calgary Flames their first Stanley Cup in 1989. Selected by the
Maple Leafs fourth overall in the 1973 Amateur Draft, McDonald spent six years
on the Toronto right wing before being traded to the Colorado Rockies, where
he was named captain, an honour he assumed again when
dealt to Calgary in 1981–82.

Selected by the Detroit Red Wings second overall in the 1971 NHL Amateur
Draft behind Guy Lafleur, Marcel Dionne went on to star with three NHL teams
for almost two decades, becoming the third-highest scorer in NHL history.
It was with the Los Angeles Kings on the "Triple Crown Line" with Dave Taylor
and Charlie Simmer that Dionne reached his scoring potential, leading the
league in 1980, and runner-up in 1977, '79 and '81.

Guy Lafleur

Back in the late 1950s and early 1960s all across Quebec, young schoolboys begged their fathers for a chance to stay up late and watch a couple of periods of the Montreal Canadiens' games. All across the province these young boys went out to the neighbourhood rinks, sticks and skates over their shoulders. They wore the bleu-blanc-rouge of the Habs and favoured the number 4 of Jean Béliveau. They emulated the moves of the Montreal captain.

With the first pick in the 1971 Amateur Draft, Montreal would choose a future NHL superstar. Playing on a franchise
with a history of outstanding offensive players, Guy Lafleur maintained that tradition, establishing himself as one
of the greatest right-wingers of all time. A three-time league-leading scorer and two-time league MVP,
Lafleur won the Conn Smythe Trophy in Montreal's 1977 Cup triumph over Boston,
one of the five Stanley Cups he won with the team.

"I was one of them," says Guy Lafleur. "During the week, on school nights, my father allowed me only to watch the first period. Then I was sent to bed. But sometimes I would hide on the staircase and watch from there. And Saturday, after playing in games or in the backyard rinks all day, I was allowed to stay up and watch the whole game. And I always wore my number 4 Canadiens sweater. Some wore number 9 [worn by Maurice Richard], but I always wore Jean Béliveau's number."

The young Lafleur was like so many others in his idolatry, but he was unique in other ways. On the sheets of ice in the backyards of Thurso, Quebec, and at the town's arena, he was the best minor hockey player in the province. In ensuing years he achieved the status of a celebrity as a schoolboy. At age 10, although he was two years younger than most of the players, Lafleur dominated competition at the Quebec peewee tournament. At 14, he went on to play junior hockey in Quebec City.

"It still seemed like a dream, very far away, to play in the Forum," Lafleur says. "I knew when I was scoring goals in peewee and bantam that I might go on to play hockey somewhere, in junior, maybe something more. But the Forum, it seemed remote. We were hockey players; they were heroes."

By age 20, in his last junior season, he shattered all scoring records in the Quebec junior league, with 130 goals and 79 assists in 62 games. In the playoffs he averaged three points a game and led the Quebec Remparts to a Memorial Cup championship. Weeks later, Montreal selected him with the first pick overall in the 1971 Amateur Draft.

It was a period of transition for the Canadiens. The team's legendary captain, Jean Béliveau, had retired following Montreal's triumph in the '71 Stanley Cup playoffs. Burdened by comparisons to nonpareil Béliveau, Lafleur struggled in his first three seasons with the Canadiens. Many fans criticized Montreal general manager Sam Pollock and believed that the team had wasted its top pick on a second-line player. "I never lost confidence," Lafleur says. "Any player on a good team needs a couple of seasons to adjust to the NHL. I knew that my time was going to come."

In Lafleur's fourth season, he made that number 1 pick look like Pollock's masterstroke and silenced the critics. The right-winger exploded for 53 goals and 66 assists, fourth in the league in scoring.

Long heralded as the next Canadiens superstar, Lafleur's record-breaking junior career
in Quebec City echoed that of Jean Béliveau. And although Béliveau offered him his
retired number 4 jersey, Lafleur instead made his own mark, as his number 10
became synonymous with yet another Montreal dynasty. Scotty Bowman,
Lafleur's coach during his best years, marvelled at the way he drove himself
to improve. Lafleur was always free to play as he wished.

Moreover, he led the team to a tie with Philadelphia and Buffalo for first overall in the 1974–75 regular-season standings. Neither Lafleur nor the Canadiens had quite reached their peaks — the Sabres knocked off Montreal in the playoffs that spring. They needed a catalyst — not a player, not a coach, but a moment that would make them great.

That moment came at the Forum on New Year's Eve of 1975: an exhibition between the Canadiens and Central Red Army of the Soviet Union. "There was nothing like that night," Lafleur says. "I played for Canada many times, and I was always proud to do that, but we wanted to show that it didn't take a team of selects to beat the Soviets. We wanted to prove that we were the best team in the world."

The Canadiens weren't playing the Soviet national team that night, but the Red Army line-up featured the best players from the other hockey super-power: Tretiak, Vasiliev, Maltsev, Mikhailov and Kharlamov, among others. Montreal took the game to Red Army and outshot the visitors 38–13. The difference in the game was goaltender Vladislav Tretiak. "We played great hockey that night," Lafleur said. "It was only Tretiak that kept Red Army in the game. We were in front 2–0 in the first period and 3–1 in the second, but Tretiak came up with so many saves to keep them in the game. When the siren went after 60 minutes and the scoreboard showed it was 3–all we skated off the ice, feeling like we had won. We had done everything we wanted to except beat Tretiak."

Lafleur points to that game as a key to the development of the Canadien team that went on to win four straight Stanley Cups in the late 70s. "We took strength from that game," he says. "We went on to beat the Flyers a few months later in the Finals and that Red Army game had a lot to do with it. It was tremendous for our confidence, not just then but for at least a couple of years afterwards. It gave us an identity."

Lafleur himself gave an identity and star quality to the best team of the era. In each of the next three seasons, Lafleur won the league scoring title and Montreal took home the Stanley Cup. Remarkably, in that three-year span the Habs lost only 29 of 240 regular-season games. "As a coach, Scotty Bowman liked to be hard on his players," Lafleur says. "In the 1976–77 season, we lost only eight games, so he had to work hard to find something to complain about and it was easy not to take the criticism to heart."

Bowman could have harped about other players, but Lafleur was above reproach. He raised the play of his linemates, Steve Shutt, the sniper on the left wing, and centremen Peter Mahovlich and Jacques Lemaire. They were stars in their own right, but Lafleur was the best in the game, peerless. Most of his goals, it seemed, were works of art, the product of his blinding speed, his puck-handling skills and an uncanny intuition. Others have notched more goals in their careers, but none have scored so many with so much flair.

On the way to Montreal's fourth consecutive Stanley Cup in the 1978–79 playoffs, the seventh game of the semifinal against Boston at the Forum provided another defining moment in Lafleur's career. With the Canadiens trailing 3–2 with less than three minutes left in regulation time, Boston was penalized for too many men on the ice. Lafleur blazed out of his own zone, received a drop pass on the right wing and wired a slapshot past Bruins goaltender Gilles Gilbert. Lafleur had always found a way to score a goal when it was needed the most. It's a tribute to Lafleur's prowess in the clutch that it seemed inevitable that he'd find a way to score down the stretch. Yvon Lambert scored the winner for the Canadiens in overtime, and Montreal easily defeated the Rangers in the final, but the sense was that Lafleur won the Cup with that slapshot from the wing against Boston.

"We were such a confident team that, even in the dressing room before the third period, there was no nervousness," Lafleur says. "No one felt that the game would get away from us or that we wouldn't win the Cup."

It turned out to be Lafleur's last taste of champagne in the bleu-blanc-rouge. The next season, Lafleur was knocked out of the playoffs with an injury in a first-round series against Hartford, and Montreal fell to Minnesota in the semifinals.

In November of 1984, Guy Lafleur announced his retirement. After his election to the Hockey Hall of Fame in 1988, he made a comeback with the Rangers. He ended his career with the Quebec Nordiques in 1991. In 17 seasons he scored 560 goals and 1,353 points. The measure of his career, however, was not statistics but transcendent moments. Although the Forum must have seemed so far away for a schoolboy in Thurso, none made the rink more his own than did Guy Lafleur.

With a skill that at times seemed supernatural, Guy
Lafleur starred with the Canadiens from 1971–72
to 1984–85, setting team scoring records that still
stand. However, his final visits to the Forum were
not as a Canadien, but as a member of the
New York Rangers and the Quebec Nordiques,
where he closed out his spectacular
career in 1990–91.

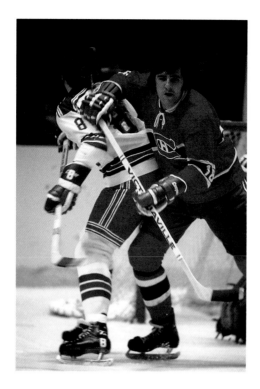

Top left: Serge Savard won seven Stanley Cups as a player and two as managing director of the Canadiens. He was an exciting defenceman, inspiring Montreal announcer Danny Gallivan to describe one of his more flamboyant moves as the "Savardian Spinarama." Bottom left: Winning 10 Stanley Cups, Yvan "The Roadrunner" Cournoyer was everything a Montreal Canadien should be.

Top right: Anatoli Tarasov, the great Russian coach, once called Bob Gainey "technically the best player in the world today." He carried the captain's C as if he had been born wearing it. Bottom right: With six Stanley Cups as an NHL coach, Scotty Bowman is also the winningest coach in NHL history. A master motivator, his teams reflect a commitment to defence combined with exciting offensive flair.

Larry Robinson was a force that exceeded his considerable size on six Montreal
Stanley Cup-winning teams. A commanding presence on the blue line, Robinson
ensured respect for all of his teammates, while winning two Norris Trophies
and one Conn Smythe for himself.

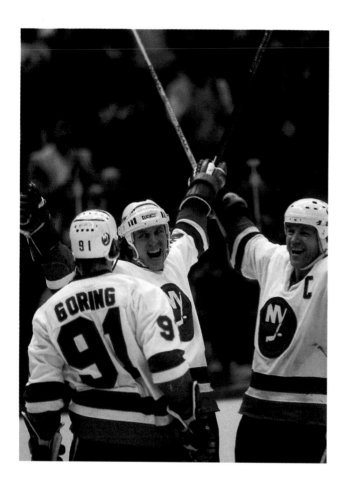

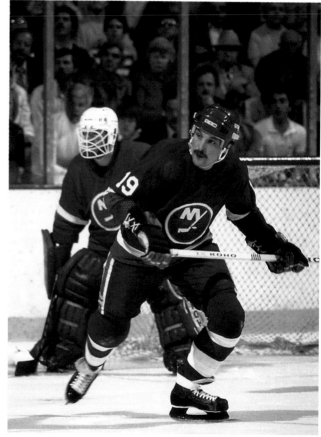

Above left: *A familiar sight, as Mike Bossy (centre)—perhaps the most natural goal scorer to ever play the game—celebrates yet another point. On an Islanders team characterized by a steady defence led by captain Denis Potvin, and gifted role-players like Butch Goring, Bossy was able to play his own game—one that led to more than 500 goals and four Stanley Cups in an injury-shortened 10-year career. Above right: Goalie Billy Smith and centre Bryan Trottier represent the heart and soul of the Islanders dynasty. Although Trottier retired sixth among all-time* NHL point leaders and Smith won a Vezina Trophy in 1982, there are no statistics to measure the leadership that Smith and Trottier brought to the Islanders. Facing page: Denis Potvin and the New York Islanders held the Stanley Cup aloft four years in a row. From 1973 to 1988 Potvin's rock-solid defence combined with record-breaking offensive abilities provided the Islanders a foundation on which to build a dynasty. During a 15-year NHL career, Potvin received the Calder Trophy as top rookie in 1974, and was three times awarded the Norris Trophy as the NHL's premier defenceman.

Members' Honour Roll

Note: Early hockey statistics are incomplete and/or unavailable prior to the formation of the National Hockey League. Statistics provided were researched from Hockey Hall of Fame archival sources including the Ernie Fitzsimmons Collection as well as newspapers, scrapbooks and recollections of early games. Every effort has been made for 100 percent accuracy. Should you have any additions or deletions, please do not hesitate to contact the Hockey Hall of Fame, BCE Place, 30 Yonge Street, Toronto, Ontario, Canada M5E 1X8 Tel (416) 360-7735 Fax (416) 360-1316.

All totals are NHL, unless otherwise indicated: • indicates non–NHL career totals.
† indicates combined NHL & non-NHL career totals. x or ——— indicates information unavailable.
RS Regular Season PO Playoffs

Players

Player	Teams		Games Played	Goals	Assists	Total Points	Penalty Minutes
ABEL, SID Melville, Saskatchewan 1918 – Inducted 1969	Pittsburgh Hornets 1938 – 39 IAHL Detroit Red Wings 1938 – 43 & 1945 – 52 NHL Indianapolis Capitols 1939 – 40 AHL Chicago Blackhawks 1952 – 53 NHL	RS PO	613 96	189 28	283 30	472 58	376 77
ADAMS, JACK Fort William, Ontario 1895 – 1968 Inducted 1959	Toronto Arenas 1917 – 19 NHL Vancouver Millionaires 1919 – 22 PCHA Toronto St. Pats 1922 – 26 NHL Ottawa Senators 1926 – 27 NHL	RS† PO†	243 28	134 11	50 x	184 11	307 12
APPS, SYL Paris, Ontario 1915 – Inducted 1961	McMaster University 1931 – 35 Hamilton Tigers 1935 – 36 OHA Toronto Maple Leafs 1936 – 43 & 1945 – 48 NHL	RS PO	423 69	201 25	231 28	432 53	56 16
ARMSTRONG, GEORGE Skead, Ontario 1930 – Inducted 1975	Toronto Marlboros 1948 – 50 OHA Toronto Maple Leafs 1949 – 50 NHL Pittsburgh Hornets 1950 – 52 AHL Toronto Maple Leafs 1951 – 71 NHL	RS PO	1187 110	296 26	417 34	713 60	721 52
BAILEY, IRVINE "ACE" Bracebridge, Ontario 1903 – 1992 Inducted 1975	St. Mary's Juniors 1921 – 23 OHA St. Mary's Seniors 1923 – 24 OHA Peterborough 1924 – 26 OHA Toronto St. Pats 1926 – 27 NHL Toronto Maple Leafs 1927 – 34 NHL	RS PO	313 20	111 3	82 4	193 7	472 12
BAIN, DAN Belleville, Ontario 1874 – 1962 Inducted 1945	Winnipeg Victorias 1894 – 97 Winnipeg Victorias 1897 – 1902 MHL	RS* PO*	x 11	x 10	x x	x x	x x
BAKER, HOBEY Wissahickon, Pennsylvania 1892 – 1918 Inducted 1945	St. Pauls High School 1906 – 10 Princeton University 1910 – 13 St. Nicholas 1913 – 16 AAHL	RS* PO	8 x	1 x	x x	1 x	x x
BARBER, BILL Callander, Ontario 1952 – Inducted 1990	Kitchener Rangers 1969 – 72 OHA Richmond Robins 1972 – 73 AHL Philadelphia Flyers 1972 – 84 NHL	RS PO	903 129	420 53	463 55	883 108	623 109
BARRY, MARTY St. Gabriel, Quebec 1905 – 1969 Inducted 1965	NY Americans 1927 – 28 NHL Boston Bruins 1929 – 35 NHL Detroit Red Wings 1935 – 39 NHL Montreal Canadiens 1939 – 40 NHL Pittsburgh Hornets 1939 – 40 AHL Minneapolis Millers 1940 – 41 AHA	RS PO	509 43	195 15	192 18	387 33	231 34
BATHGATE, ANDY Winnipeg, Manitoba 1932 – Inducted 1978	Guelph Biltmores 1949 – 52 OHA NY Rangers 1952 – 64 NHL Vancouver Canucks 1952 – 54 & 1968 – 70 WHL Cleveland Barons 1953 – 54 AHL Toronto Maple Leafs 1963 – 65 NHL Detroit Red Wings 1965 – 67 NHL Pittsburgh Hornets 1966 – 67 AHL Pittsburgh Penguins 1967 – 68 & 1970 – 71 NHL Vancouver Blazers 1974 – 75 WHA	RS PO	1069 54	349 21	624 14	973 35	624 76
BÉLIVEAU, JEAN Trois Rivières, Quebec 1931 – Inducted 1972	Quebec Citadelles 1949 – 51 QJHL Montreal Canadiens 1950 – 51 & 1952 – 71 NHL Quebec Aces 1951 – 53 QSHL	RS PO	1125 162	507 79	712 97	1219 176	1029 211
BENTLEY, DOUG Delisle, Saskatchewan 1916 – 1972 Inducted 1964	Drumheller Minors 1937 – 39 SSHL Chicago Blackhawks 1939 – 44 & 1945 – 52 NHL Saskatoon Quakers 1951 – 54 WHL NY Rangers 1953 – 54 NHL	RS PO	566 23	219 9	324 8	543 17	217 12
BENTLEY, MAX Delisle, Saskatchewan 1920 – 1984 Inducted 1966	Providence Reds 1940 – 41 AHL Kansas City Americans 1940 – 41 AHA Chicago Blackhawks 1940 – 43 & 1945 – 48 NHL Toronto Maple Leafs 1947 – 53 NHL NY Rangers 1953 – 54 NHL	RS PO	646 52	245 18	299 27	544 45	175 14
BLAKE, HECTOR "TOE" Victoria Mines, Ontario 1912 – 1995 Inducted 1966	Hamilton Tigers 1932 – 35 OHA Montreal Maroons 1934 – 35 NHL Providence Reds 1935 – 36 CAHL Montreal Canadiens 1935 – 48 NHL	RS PO	578 57	235 25	292 37	527 62	272 23
BOIVIN, LEO Prescott, Ontario 1932 – Inducted 1986	Pittsburgh Hornets 1951 – 52 AHL Toronto Maple Leafs 1951 – 55 AHL Boston Bruins 1954 – 66 NHL Detroit Red Wings 1965 – 67 NHL Pittsburgh Penguins 1967 – 69 NHL Minnesota North Stars 1968 – 70 NHL	RS PO	1150 54	72 3	250 10	322 13	1192 59
BOON, DICKIE Belleville, Ontario 1878 – 1961 Inducted 1952	Montreal AAA's 1899 – 1903 CAHL Montreal Wanderers 1904 – 06 FAHL	RS* PO*	42 7	10 x	x x	10 x	x x
BOSSY, MIKE Montreal, Quebec 1957 – Inducted 1991	Laval National 1972 – 77 QJHL NY Islanders 1977 – 87 NHL	RS PO	752 129	573 85	553 75	1126 160	210 38

Players	Teams		Games Played	Goals	Assists	Total Points	Penalty Minutes
OUCHARD, BUTCH Montreal, Quebec 920 – nducted 1966	Verdun Maple Leafs 1937 – 40 QJHL Montreal Canadiens 1940 – 41 QJHL Montreal Canadiens 1941 – 56 NHL	RS PO	785 113	49 11	144 21	193 32	863 121
OUCHER, FRANK ttawa, Ontario 901 – 1977 nducted 1958	Ottawa Senators 1921 – 22 NHL Vancouver Maroons 1922 – 24 PCHA Vancouver Maroons 1924 – 26 WCHL NY Rangers 1926 – 38 & 1943 – 44 NHL	RS PO	557 56	161 16	262 18	423 34	119 12
OUCHER, GEORGE ttawa, Ontario 896 – 1960 nducted 1960	Ottawa Senators 1915 – 17 NHA Ottawa Senators 1917 – 29 NHL Montreal Maroons 1928 – 31 NHL Chicago Blackhawks 1931 – 32 NHL	RS PO	457 44	122 11	62 4	184 15	739 84
OWIE, RUSSELL "DUBBIE" Montreal, Quebec 880 – 1959 nducted 1945	Montreal Victorias 1898 – 1905 CAHL Montreal Victorias 1905 – 08 ECAHA Montreal Victorias 1908 – 10 IPAHU	RS* PO*	80 4	234 1	x x	234 1	x x
BROADBENT, HARRY "PUNCH" Ottawa, Ontario 892 – 1971 nducted 1962	Ottawa Senators 1912 – 15 NHA Ottawa Senators 1918 – 24 & 1927 – 28 NHL Montreal Maroons 1924 – 27 NHL NY Americans 1928 – 29 NHL	RS PO	302 41	122 13	45 3	167 16	553 69
BUCYK, JOHNNY Edmonton, Alberta 1935 – Inducted 1981	Edmonton Flyers 1953 – 56 WHL Detroit Red Wings 1955 – 57 NHL Boston Bruins 1957 – 78 NHL	RS PO	1540 124	556 41	813 62	1369 103	497 42
BURCH, BILLY Yonkers, New York 1900 – 1950 Inducted 1974	Toronto Aura Lee 1920 – 22 OHA Hamilton Tigers 1922 – 25 NHL NY Americans 1925 – 32 NHL Boston/Chicago 1932 – 33 NHL	RS PO	390 2	137 0	53 0	190 0	251 0
CAMERON, HARRY Pembroke, Ontario 1890 – 1953 Inducted 1962	Toronto Blueshirts 1912 – 16 NHA Montreal Wanderers 1916 – 17 NHA Toronto Arenas 1917 – 19 NHL Ottawa Senators 1918 – 19 NHL Montreal Canadiens 1919 – 20 NHL Toronto St. Pats 1919 – 23 NHL Saskatoon Crescents 1923 – 25 WCHL Saskatoon Crescents 1925 – 26 WCHL	RS† PO†	312 28	174 9	27 1	201 10	154 29
CLANCY, FRANCIS "KING" Ottawa, Ontario 1903 – 1986 Inducted 1958	Ottawa St. Brigids 1918 – 21 SR. Ottawa Senators 1921 – 30 NHL Toronto Maple Leafs 1930 – 37 NHL	RS PO	592 61	137 9	143 8	280 17	904 92
CLAPPER, AUBREY "DIT" Newmarket, Ontario 1907 – 1978 Inducted 1947	Toronto Parkdales 1925 – 26 OHA Boston Tigers 1926 – 27 CAHL Boston Bruins 1927 – 47 NHL	RS PO	833 86	228 13	246 17	474 30	462 50
CLARKE, BOBBY Flin Flon, Manitoba 1949 – Inducted 1987	Flin Flon Bombers 1967 – 69 WHL Philadelphia Flyers 1969 – 84 NHL	RS PO	1144 136	358 42	852 77	1210 119	1453 152
CLEGHORN, SPRAGUE Montreal, Quebec 1890 – 1956 Inducted 1958	Ren. Cream. Kings 1910 – 11 NHA Montreal Wanderers 1911 – 17 NHA Ottawa Senators 1918 – 21 NHL Toronto St. Pats 1920 – 21 NHL Montreal Canadiens 1921 – 25 NHL Boston Bruins 1925 – 28 NHL	RS† PO†	377 41	163 6	39 9	202 15	489 48
COLVILLE, NEIL Edmonton, Alberta 1914 – 1987 Inducted 1967	NY Rangers 1935 – 42 & 1944 – 49 NHL Philadelphia Ramblers 1935 – 36 CAHL New Haven Ramblers 1948 – 50 AHL	RS PO	464 46	99 7	166 19	265 26	213 33
CONACHER, CHARLIE Toronto, Ontario 1909 – 1967 Inducted 1961	Toronto Marlboros 1927 – 29 OHA Toronto Maple Leafs 1929 – 38 NHL Detroit Red Wings 1938 – 39 NHL NY Americans 1939 – 41 NHL	RS PO	460 49	225 17	173 18	398 35	523 53
CONACHER, LIONEL "BIG TRAIN" Toronto, Ontario 1900 – 1954 Inducted 1994	Toronto Aura Lee 1917 – 19 JR. Toronto Canoe Club 1919 – 20 JR. OHA Toronto Aura Lee 1920 – 22 SR. OHA Pittsburgh Yellow Jackets 1923 – 25 SR. USAHA Pittsburgh Pirates 1925 – 27 NHL New York Americans 1927 – 30 NHL Montreal Maroons 1930 – 33 & 1934 – 37 NHL Chicago Blackhawks 1933 – 34 NHL	RS† PO†	584 58	115 16	107 4	222 20	882 34
COOK, BILL Brantford, Ontario 1896 – 1986 Inducted 1952	Saskatoon Crescents 1922 – 25 WCHL Saskatoon Crescents 1925 – 26 WHL NY Rangers 1926 – 37 NHL	RS PO	586 50	322 15	196 12	518 27	483 66
COOK, FREDERICK "BUN" Kingston, Ontario 1903 – Inducted 1995	Soo Greyhounds 1923 – 24 NOHA Saskatoon Sheiks 1924 –25 WHL New York Rangers 1926 – 36 NHL Boston Bruins 1936 – 37 NHL	RS PO	473 46	158 15	144 3	302 18	427 57
COULTER, ART Winnipeg, Manitoba 1909 – Inducted 1974	Philadelphia Arrows 1929 – 32 CAHL Chicago Blackhawks 1931 – 36 NHL NY Rangers 1935 – 42 NHL	RS PO	465 49	30 4	82 5	112 9	543 61
COURNOYER, YVAN Drummondville, Quebec 1943 – Inducted 1982	Montreal Canadiens 1961 – 64 OHA Montreal Canadiens 1963 – 79 NHL Quebec Aces 1964 – 65 AHL	RS PO	968 147	428 64	435 63	863 127	255 47
COWLEY, BILL Bristol, Quebec 1912 – 1993 Inducted 1968	St. Louis Eagles 1934 – 35 NHL Boston Bruins 1935 – 47 NHL	RS PO	549 64	195 13	353 33	548 46	143 22
CRAWFORD, RUSTY Cardinal, Ontario 1885 – 1971 Inducted 1962	Quebec Bulldogs 1912 – 17 NHA Toronto Arenas 1917 – 19 NHL Ottawa Senators 1917 – 18 NHL Saskatoon Sheiks 1921 – 23 WCHL Calgary Tigers 1922 – 25 WCHL Vancouver Maroons 1925 – 26 WHL Minneapolis Millers 1926 – 30 AHA	RS† PO†	245 15	110 6	3 1	113 7	51 0
DARRAGH, JACK Ottawa, Ontario 1890 – 1924 Inducted 1962	Ottawa Senators 1910 – 17 NHA Ottawa Senators 1917 – 24 NHL	RS† PO†	250 30	194 19	21 2	215 21	88 7
DAVIDSON, ALLAN "SCOTTY" Kingston, Ontario 1890 – 1915 Inducted 1950	Kingston Frontenacs 1909 – 11 OHA Toronto Parkdales 1911 – 12 OHA Toronto Blueshirts 1912 – 14 NHA	RS* PO*	40 4	42 3	13 x	55 3	133 x
DAY, CLARENCE "HAPPY" Owen Sound, Ontario 1901 – 1990 Inducted 1961	Hamilton Tigers 1922 – 24 OHA Toronto St. Pats 1924 – 26 NHL Toronto Maple Leafs 1926 – 37 NHL NY Americans 1937 – 38 NHL	RS PO	581 53	86 4	116 7	202 11	602 56
DELVECCHIO, ALEX Fort William, Ontario 1931 – Inducted 1977	Oshawa Generals 1950 – 51 OHA Detroit Red Wings 1950 – 74 NHL Indianapolis Capitols 1951 – 52 AHL	RS PO	1549 121	456 35	825 69	1281 104	383 29
DENNENY, CY Farran's Point, Ontario 1897 – 1970 Inducted 1959	Toronto Shamrocks 1914 – 15 NHA Toronto Arenas 1915 – 16 NHA Ottawa Senators 1916 – 17 NHA Ottawa Senators 1917 – 28 NHL Boston Bruins 1928 – 29 NHL	RS† PO†	368 43	281 19	69 3	350 22	210 31
DIONNE, MARCEL Drummondville, Quebec 1951 – Inducted 1992	St. Catharines Black Hawks 1969 – 71 OHA Detroit Red Wings 1971 – 75 NHL LA Kings 1975 – 87 NHL NY Rangers 1987 – 89 NHL Denver Rangers 1988 – 89 IHL	RS PO	1348 49	731 21	1040 24	1771 45	600 17
DRILLON, GORDIE Moncton, New Brunswick 1914 – 1986 Inducted 1975	Toronto Maple Leafs 1936 – 42 NHL Montreal Canadiens 1942 – 43 NHL	RS PO	311 50	155 26	139 15	294 41	56 10

Players			Games Played	Goals	Assists	Total Points	Penalty Minutes
DRINKWATER, GRAHAM Montreal, Quebec 1875 – 1946 Inducted 1950	Montreal AAA's 1892 – 93 AHA Montreal Victorias 1893, 1895 – 98 AHA McGill University 1894 – 95 Montreal Victorias 1899 CAHL	RS* PO*	37 4	40 2	x x	40 2	x x
DUMART, WOODY Kitchener, Ontario 1916 – Inducted 1992	Kitchener Waterloo Greenshirts 1934 – 35 OHA Boston Cubs 1935 – 36 CAHL Providence Reds 1936 – 37 IAHL Boston Bruins 1935 – 42 & 1945 – 54 NHL RCAF Flyers 1942 – 43 Providence Reds 1954 – 55 AHL	RS PO	771 88	211 12	218 15	429 27	99 23
DUNDERDALE, TOMMY Benella, Australia 1887 – 1960 Inducted 1974	Winnipeg Victorias 1906 – 09 MHL Montreal Shamrocks 1909 – 10 NHA Quebec Bulldogs 1910 – 11 NHA Victoria Aristocrats 1911 – 15 & 1918 – 23 PCHA Portland Rosebuds 1915 – 18 PCHA Saskatoon/Edmonton 1923 – 24 WCHL	RS* PO*	290 12	225 6	x x	225 6	x x
DUTTON, MERVYN "RED" Russell, Manitoba 1898 – 1987 Inducted 1958	Calgary Tigers 1921 – 26 WCHL Montreal Maroons 1926 – 30 NHL NY Americans 1930 – 36 NHL	RS PO	449 18	29 1	67 0	96 1	871 33
DYE, CECIL "BABE" Hamilton, Ontario 1898 – 1962 Inducted 1970	Toronto St. Pats 1919 – 26 NHL Hamilton Tigers 1920 – 21 NHL Chicago Blackhawks 1926 – 28 NHL NY Americans 1928 – 29 NHL Toronto Maple Leafs 1930 – 31 NHL	RS PO	270 15	202 11	41 2	243 13	190 11
ESPOSITO, PHIL Sault Ste. Marie, Ontario 1942 – Inducted 1984	St. Catharines Tee Pees 1961 – 62 OHA Sault Ste. Marie Thunderbirds 1961 – 62 EPHL St. Louis Braves 1962 – 64 EPHL Chicago Blackhawks 1963 – 67 NHL Boston Bruins 1967 – 76 NHL NY Rangers 1975 – 81 NHL	RS PO	1282 130	717 61	873 76	1590 137	910 137
FARRELL, ARTHUR Montreal, Quebec 1877 – 1909 Inducted 1965	Montreal Shamrocks 1896 – 97 AHA Montreal Shamrocks 1898 – 1901 CAHL	RS* PO*	26 8	29 13	x x	29 13	x x
FLAMAN, FERNIE Dysart, Saskatchewan 1927 – Inducted 1990	Boston Bruins 1944 – 51 & 1954 – 61 NHL Hershey Bears 1946 – 47 AHL Toronto Maple Leafs 1950 – 54 NHL Providence Reds 1961 – 64 AHL	RS PO	910 63	34 4	174 8	208 12	1370 93
FOYSTON, FRANK Minesing, Ontario 1891 – 1966 Inducted 1958	Toronto Blueshirts 1912 – 16 NHA Seattle Metros 1915 – 24 PCHA Victoria Aristocrats 1924 – 26 WCHL Detroit Cougars 1926 – 28 NHL	RS† PO†	357 19	242 14	7 x	249 14	32 x
FREDRICKSON, FRANK Winnipeg, Manitoba 1895 – 1979 Inducted 1958	Winnipeg Falcons 1913 – 20 MHL Victoria Cougars 1920 – 24 PCHA Victoria Cougars 1924 – 26 WCHL Boston Bruins 1926 – 29 NHL Detroit Falcons 1926 – 27 & 1930 – 31 NHL Pittsburgh Pirates 1928 – 30 NHL	RS† PO†	327 28	170 13	34 5	204 18	206 26
GADSBY, BILL Calgary, Alberta 1927 – Inducted 1970	Edmonton Canadians 1944 – 46 JR. Kansas City Play-Mors 1946 – 47 USHL Chicago Blackhawks 1946 – 55 NHL NY Rangers 1954 – 61 NHL Detroit Red Wings 1961 – 66 NHL	RS PO	1248 67	130 4	437 23	567 27	1539 92
GAINEY, BOB Peterborough, Ontario 1953 – Inducted 1992	Peterborough Petes 1970 – 73 OHA Nova Scotia Voyageurs 1973 – 74 AHL Montreal Canadiens 1973 – 89 NHL	RS PO	1160 182	239 25	262 48	501 73	585 151
GARDINER, HERB Winnipeg, Manitoba 1891 – 1972 Inducted 1958	Calgary Tigers 1921 – 26 WCHL Montreal Canadiens 1926 – 29 NHL Chicago Blackhawks 1928 – 29 NHL	RS† PO†	233 20	44 3	9 1	53 4	52 10

Players			Games Played	Goals	Assists	Total Points	Penalty Minutes
GARDNER, JIMMY Montreal, Quebec 1881 – 1940 Inducted 1962	Montreal AAA's 1900 – 03 CAHL Montreal Wanderers 1903 – 04 FAHL Montreal Shamrocks 1907 – 08 ECAHA Montreal Wanderers 1908 – 09 ECHA Montreal Wanderers 1909 – 11 NHA New Westminster Royals 1911 – 13 PCHA Montreal Canadiens 1913 – 15 NHA	RS* PO*	112 9	63 2	x x	63 2	x x
GEOFFRION, BERNIE "BOOM BOOM" Montreal, Quebec 1931 – Inducted 1972	Montreal Royals 1948 – 50 QSHL Montreal Canadiens 1950 – 64 NHL NY Rangers 1966 – 68 NHL	RS PO	883 132	393 58	429 60	822 118	689 88
GERARD, EDDIE Ottawa, Ontario 1890 – 1937 Inducted 1945	Ottawa Victorias 1907 – 08 FAHL Ottawa New Edinburghs 1910 – 14 OCHL Ottawa Senators 1913 – 17 NHA Ottawa Senators 1917 – 23 NHL Toronto St. Patricks 1921 – 22 NHL	RS† PO†	201 35	93 9	30 1	123 10	106 52
GILBERT, ROD Montreal, Quebec 1941 – Inducted 1982	Guelph Biltmores 1957 – 60 OHA Trois Rivières Lions 1959 – 60 EPHL Kitchener-Waterloo Beavers 1961 – 62 EPHL NY Rangers 1960 – 78 NHL	RS PO	1065 79	406 34	615 33	1021 67	508 43
GILMOUR, BILLY Ottawa, Ontario 1885 – 1959 Inducted 1962	Ottawa Senators 1902 – 04 CAHL Ottawa Senators 1904 – 05 FAHL Ottawa Senators 1905 – 06 ECAHA Montreal Victorias 1907 – 08 ECAHA Ottawa Senators 1908 – 09 ECHA Ottawa Senators 1915 – 16 NHA	RS* PO*	32 9	26 7	x x	26 7	x x
GOHEEN, FRANK "MOOSE" White Bear Lake, Minnesota 1894 – 1979 Inducted 1952	St. Paul Athletic Club 1914 – 25 Buffalo 1930 – 31 AHA St. Paul Saints 1925 – 33 AHA	RS* PO*	260 23	77 6	39 3	116 9	325 20
GOODFELLOW "EBBIE" Ottawa, Ontario 1907 – 1985 Inducted 1963	Detroit Olympics 1928 – 29 CPHL Detroit Cougars 1929 – 30 NHL Detroit Falcons 1930 – 33 NHL Detroit Red Wings 1933 – 43 NHL	RS PO	554 45	134 8	190 8	324 16	511 65
GRANT, MIKE Montreal, Quebec 1874 – 1961 Inducted 1950	Montreal Victorias 1893 – 98 AHA Montreal Victorias 1898 – 1900 & 1901 – 02 CAHL Montreal Shamrocks 1900 – 01 CAHL	RS* PO*	55 8	10 0	x x	10 0	x x
GREEN, WILF "SHORTY" Sudbury, Ontario 1896 – 1960 Inducted 1962	Sudbury Wolves 1919 – 23 NOHA Hamilton Tigers 1923 – 25 NHL NY Americans 1925 – 27 NHL	RS PO	103 0	33 0	8 0	41 0	151 0
GRIFFIS, SI Onaga, Kansas 1883 – 1950 Inducted 1950	Rat Portage Thistles 1902 – 05 MNSHA Kenora Thistles 1905 – 07 MHL Vancouver Millionaires 1911 – 19 PCHA	RS* PO*	117 18	39 5	x x	39 5	x x
HALL, JOE Staffordshire, England 1882 – 1919 Inducted 1961	Brandon 1900 – 05 MHL Quebec Bulldogs 1905 – 06 ECAHA Brandon 1906 – 07 MHL Montreal AAA's 1907 – 08 ECAHA Montreal Shamrocks 1907 – 08 ECAHA Montreal Wanderers 1908 – 09 ECHA Montreal Shamrocks 1909 – 10 NHA Quebec Bulldogs 1910 – 17 NHA Montreal Canadiens 1917 – 19 NHL	RS† PO†	198 22	105 9	1 2	106 11	145 31
HARVEY, DOUG Montreal, Quebec 1924 – 1989 Inducted 1973	Montreal Royals 1942 – 47 QSHL Buffalo Bisons 1947 – 48 AHL Montreal Canadiens 1947 – 61 NHL NY Rangers 1961 – 64 NHL St. Paul Rangers 1963 – 64 CPHL Quebec Aces 1963 – 65 AHL Baltimore Clippers 1965 – 67 AHL Pittsburgh Hornets 1966 – 67 AHL Detroit Red Wings 1966 – 67 NHL Kansas City Blues 1967 – 68 CPHL St. Louis Blues 1967 – 69 NHL	RS PO	1113 137	88 8	452 64	540 72	1216 152

AY, GEORGE
istowel, Ontario
898 – 1975
nducted 1958

Regina Capitals 1921 – 25 WCHL
Portland Capitals 1925 – 26 WHL
Chicago Blackhawks 1926 – 27 NHL
Detroit Cougars 1927 – 30 NHL
Detroit Falcons 1930 – 31 NHL
Detroit Red Wings 1932 – 34 NHL

	Games Played	Goals	Assists	Total Points	Penalty Minutes
RS†	373	179	60	239	84
PO†	18	5	3	8	2

HEXTALL, BRYAN
Grenfell, Saskatchewan
1913 – 1984
Inducted 1969

Vancouver Lions 1933 – 36 NWHL
NY Rangers 1936 – 44 & 1945 – 48 NHL

	Games Played	Goals	Assists	Total Points	Penalty Minutes
RS	447	187	175	362	227
PO	37	8	9	17	19

HOOPER, TOM
Kenora, Ontario
883 – 1960
Inducted 1962

Rat Portage Thistles 1901 – 05 MNSHA
Kenora Thistles 1906 – 07 MHL
Montreal Wanderers 1907 – 08 ECAHA
Montreal AAA's 1907 – 08 ECAHA

	Games Played	Goals	Assists	Total Points	Penalty Minutes
RS*	11	12	x	12	x
PO*	12	6	x	6	x

HORNER, G. REGINALD "RED"
Lynden, Ontario
1909 –
Inducted 1965

Toronto Marlboros 1925 – 29 OHA
Toronto Maple Leafs 1928 – 40 NHL

	Games Played	Goals	Assists	Total Points	Penalty Minutes
RS	490	42	110	152	1264
PO	71	7	10	17	160

HORTON, TIM
Cochrane, Ontario
1930 – 1974
Inducted 1977

Toronto St. Michael's 1947 – 49 OHA
Pittsburgh 1949 – 52 AHL
Toronto Maple Leafs 1949 – 70 NHL
NY Rangers 1969 – 71 NHL
Pittsburgh Penguins 1971 – 72 NHL
Buffalo Sabres 1972 – 74 NHL

	Games Played	Goals	Assists	Total Points	Penalty Minutes
RS	1446	115	403	518	1611
PO	126	11	39	50	183

HOWE, GORDIE
Floral, Saskatchewan
1928 –
Inducted 1972

Galt Red Wings 1944 – 45 OHA
Omaha 1945 – 46 USHL
Detroit Red Wings 1946 – 71 NHL
Houston Aeros 1973 – 77 WHA
New England Whalers 1977 – 79 WHA
Hartford Whalers 1979 – 80 NHL

	Games Played	Goals	Assists	Total Points	Penalty Minutes
RS	1767	801	1049	1850	1685
PO	157	68	92	160	220

HOWE, SYD
Ottawa, Ontario
1911 – 1976
Inducted 1965

London Panthers 1929 – 30 IHL
Ottawa Senators 1929 – 30 & 1932 – 34 NHL
Philadelphia Quakers 1930 – 31 NHL
Toronto Maple Leafs 1931 – 32 NHL
St. Louis Eagles 1934 – 35 NHL
Detroit Red Wings 1934 – 46 NHL

	Games Played	Goals	Assists	Total Points	Penalty Minutes
RS	691	237	291	528	214
PO	70	17	27	44	10

HOWELL, HARRY
Hamilton, Ontario
1932 –
Inducted 1979

Guelph Biltmores 1949 – 52 OHA
Cincinnati Mohawks 1951 – 52 AHL
NY Rangers 1952 – 69 NHL
Oakland Seals 1969 – 70 NHL
California Golden Seals 1970 – 71 NHL
LA Kings 1970 – 73 NHL
New Jersey Knights 1973 – 74 WHA
San Diego Mariners 1974 – 75 WHA
Calgary Cowboys 1975 – 76 WHA

	Games Played	Goals	Assists	Total Points	Penalty Minutes
RS	1411	94	324	418	1298
PO	38	3	3	6	32

HULL, ROBERT (BOBBY)
Pointe Anne, Ontario
1939 –
Inducted 1983

St. Catharines Tee Pees 1955 – 57 OHA
Chicago Blackhawks 1957 – 72 NHL
Winnipeg Jets 1972 – 79 WHA
Winnipeg Jets 1979 – 80 NHL
Hartford Whalers 1979 – 80 NHL

	Games Played	Goals	Assists	Total Points	Penalty Minutes
RS	1063	610	560	1170	640
PO	119	62	67	129	102

HYLAND, HARRY
Montreal, Quebec
1889 – 1969
Inducted 1962

Montreal Shamrocks 1906 – 08 CAHL
Montreal Shamrocks 1908 – 09 ECHA
Montreal Wanderers 1909 – 11 & 1912 – 17 NHA
New Westminster Royals 1911 – 12 PCHA
Montreal/Ottawa 1917 – 18 NHL

	Games Played	Goals	Assists	Total Points	Penalty Minutes
RS†	157	199	x	199	9
PO†	3	3	x	3	x

IRVIN, DICK
Limestone Ridge, Ontario
1892 – 1957
Inducted 1958

Winnipeg Monarchs 1911 – 16 MSHL
Portland Rosebuds 1916 – 17 PCHA
Regina Capitals 1921 – 25 WCHL
Portland Capitals 1925 – 26 WHL
Chicago Blackhawks 1926 – 29 NHL

	Games Played	Goals	Assists	Total Points	Penalty Minutes
RS†	249	152	23	174	76
PO†	12	6	x	6	0

JACKSON, HARVEY
Toronto, Ontario
1911 – 1966
Inducted 1971

Toronto Marlboros 1926 – 29 OHA
Toronto Maple Leafs 1929 – 39 NHL
NY Americans 1939 – 41 NHL
Boston Bruins 1941 – 44 NHL

	Games Played	Goals	Assists	Total Points	Penalty Minutes
RS	636	241	234	475	437
PO	72	18	12	30	55

JOHNSON, IVAN WILFRED "CHING"
Winnipeg, Manitoba
1897 – 1979
Inducted 1958

Minneapolis Millers 1923 – 26 USAHA
NY Rangers 1926 – 37 NHL
NY Americans 1937 – 38 NHL

	Games Played	Goals	Assists	Total Points	Penalty Minutes
RS	435	38	48	86	808
PO	60	5	2	7	159

JOHNSON, ERNIE
Montreal, Quebec
1886 – 1963
Inducted 1952

Montreal AAA's 1903 – 05 CAHL
Montreal Wanderers 1905 – 08 ECAHA
Montreal Wanderers 1908 – 09 ECHA
Montreal Wanderers 1909 – 11 NHA
New Westminster Royals 1911 – 14 PCHA
Portland Rosebuds 1914 – 18 PCHA
Victoria Aristocrats 1918 – 22 PCHA

	Games Played	Goals	Assists	Total Points	Penalty Minutes
RS*	270	123	x	123	x
PO*	21	20	x	123	x

JOHNSON, TOM
Baldur, Manitoba
1928 –
Inducted 1970

Montreal Royals 1947 – 48 QSHL
Montreal Canadiens 1947 – 48 & 1949 – 63 NHL
Buffalo Bisons 1947 – 50 AHL
Boston Bruins 1963 – 65 NHL

	Games Played	Goals	Assists	Total Points	Penalty Minutes
RS	978	51	213	264	960
PO	111	8	15	23	109

JOLIAT, AURÈLE
Ottawa, Ontario
1901 – 1986
Inducted 1947

Aberdeen 1916 – 17 OCHL
Ottawa New Edinburgh 1917 – 19 OCHL
Iroquois Falls 1919 – 21 ———
Montreal Canadiens 1922 – 38 NHL

	Games Played	Goals	Assists	Total Points	Penalty Minutes
RS	654	270	190	460	752
PO	54	14	19	33	89

KEATS, GORDON "DUKE"
Montreal, Quebec
1895 – 1972
Inducted 1958

Toronto Blueshirts 1915 – 17 NHA
Edmonton Eskimos 1921 – 25 WCHL
Edmonton Eskimos 1925 – 26 WHL
Boston & Detroit 1926 – 27 NHL
Detroit & Chicago 1927 – 28 NHL
Chicago Blackhawks 1928 – 29 NHL

	Games Played	Goals	Assists	Total Points	Penalty Minutes
RS†	256	183	19	202	112
PO†	8	2	x	2	x

KELLY, LEONARD "RED"
Simcoe, Ontario
1927 –
Inducted 1969

Toronto St. Michael's 1944 – 47 OHA
Detroit Red Wings 1947 – 60 NHL
Toronto Maple Leafs 1959 – 67 NHL

	Games Played	Goals	Assists	Total Points	Penalty Minutes
RS	1316	281	542	823	327
PO	164	33	59	92	51

KENNEDY, TED "TEEDER"
Humberstone, Ontario
1925 –
Inducted 1966

Port Colborne Sailors 1942 – 43 OHA
Toronto Maple Leafs 1942 – 55 & 1956 – 57 NHL

	Games Played	Goals	Assists	Total Points	Penalty Minutes
RS	696	231	329	560	432
PO	78	29	31	60	32

KEON, DAVE
Noranda, Quebec
1940 –
Inducted 1986

Toronto St. Michael's 1956 – 60 OHA
Sudbury Wolves 1959 – 60 EPHL
Toronto Maple Leafs 1960 – 75 NHL
Indianapolis Racers 1975 – 76 WHA
Minneapolis Saints 1975 – 77 WHA
New England Whalers 1976 – 79 WHA
Hartford Whalers 1979 – 82 NHL

	Games Played	Goals	Assists	Total Points	Penalty Minutes
RS	1296	396	590	986	117
PO	92	32	36	68	6

LACH, ELMER
Nokomis, Saskatchewan
1918 –
Inducted 1966

Moosejaw Millers 1938 – 40 SSHL
Montreal Canadiens 1940 – 54 NHL

	Games Played	Goals	Assists	Total Points	Penalty Minutes
RS	664	215	408	623	478
PO	76	19	45	64	36

LAFLEUR, GUY
Thurso, Quebec
1951 –
Inducted 1988

Quebec Aces 1966 – 69 QJHL
Quebec Remparts 1969 – 71 QJHL
Montreal Canadiens 1971 – 85 NHL
NY Rangers 1988 – 89 NHL
Quebec Nordiques 1989 – 91 NHL

	Games Played	Goals	Assists	Total Points	Penalty Minutes
RS	1126	560	793	1353	399
PO	128	58	76	134	67

LALONDE, EDOUARD "NEWSY"
Cornwall, Ontario
1887 – 1971
Inducted 1950

Cornwall 1904 – 05 FAHL
Portage Lakes 1907 – 08 MHL
Toronto Maple Leafs 1907 – 09 OPHL
Montreal & Renfrew 1909 – 10 NHA
Montreal Canadiens 1910 – 11 & 1912 – 17 NHA
Vancouver Millionaires 1911 – 12 PCHA
Montreal Canadiens 1917 – 22 NHL
Saskatoon Crescents 1922 – 25 WCHL
Saskatoon Crescents 1925 – 26 WHL
NY Americans 1926 – 27 NHL

	Games Played	Goals	Assists	Total Points	Penalty Minutes
RS†	315	428	27	455	122
PO†	29	27	1	28	19

LAPERRIÈRE, JACQUES
Rouyn, Quebec
1941 –
Inducted 1987

Ottawa – Hull Canadiens 1959 – 63 EPHL
Montreal Canadiens 1962 – 74 NHL

	Games Played	Goals	Assists	Total Points	Penalty Minutes
RS	691	40	242	282	674
PO	88	9	22	31	101

Players

LAVIOLETTE, JACK
Belleville, Ontario
1879 – 1960
Inducted 1962

Montreal Nationals 1903 – 04 FAHL
Michigan Soo 1904 – 07 IPHL
Montreal Shamrocks 1907 – 08 ECAHA
Montreal Shamrocks 1908 – 09 ECHA
Montreal Canadiens 1909 – 17 NHA
Montreal Canadiens 1917 – 18 NHL

	Games Played	Goals	Assists	Total Points	Penalty Minutes
RS†	178	58	0	58	0
PO†	14	1	0	1	0

LAPOINTE, GUY
Montreal, Quebec
1948 –
Inducted 1993

Verdun 1965 – 67 QJHL
Montreal Canadiens 1967 – 68 OHA
Houston Apollos 1968 – 69 CHL
Montreal Voyageurs 1969 – 70 AHL
Montreal Canadiens 1968 – 82 NHL
St. Louis Blues 1982 – 83 NHL
Boston Bruins 1983 – 84 NHL

	GP	G	A	PTS	PIM
RS†	1094	200	536	736	1358
PO†	145	31	56	86	190

LAPRADE, EDGAR
Mine Centre, Ontario
1919 –
Inducted 1993

Port Arthur Juniors 1935 – 38 TBHL
Port Arthur 1938 – 39 TBHL
Port Arthur Bearcats 1938 – 39 MJHL
Port Arthur Bearcats 1939 – 43 TBHL
Winnipeg Army 1943 – 44 WPG. SERV.
Barriefield Bears – Kingston
1944 – 45 SR. KCHL
New York Rangers 1945 – 55 NHL

	GP	G	A	PTS	PIM
RS†	639	281	314	595	82
PO†	56	40	32	72	21

LEMAIRE, JACQUES
LaSalle, Quebec
1945 –
Inducted 1984

Montreal Canadiens 1963 – 66 OHA
Quebec Aces 1964 – 65 AHL
Houston Apollos 1966 – 67 CPHL
Montreal Canadiens 1967 – 79 NHL

	GP	G	A	PTS	PIM
RS	853	366	469	835	217
PO	145	61	78	139	63

LEWIS, HERBIE
Calgary, Alberta
1907 –
Inducted 1989

Duluth Hornets 1924 – 28 AHA
Detroit Cougars 1928 – 30 NHL
Detroit Falcons 1930 – 33 NHL
Detroit Red Wings 1933 – 39 NHL

	GP	G	A	PTS	PIM
RS	484	148	161	309	248
PO	38	13	10	23	6

LINDSAY, TED
Renfrew, Ontario
1925 –
Inducted 1966

Toronto St. Michael's 1943 – 44 OHA
Oshawa Generals 1943 – 44 OHA
Detroit Red Wings 1944 – 57 &
1964 – 65 NHL
Chicago Blackhawks 1957 – 60 NHL

	GP	G	A	PTS	PIM
RS	1068	379	472	851	1808
PO	133	47	49	96	194

MACKAY, MICKEY
Chesley, Ontario
1894 – 1940
Inducted 1952

Vancouver Millionaires 1914 – 19 &
1920 – 24 PCHA
Vancouver Maroons 1924 – 25 WCHL
Vancouver Maroons 1925 – 26 WHL
Chicago Blackhawks 1926 – 28 NHL
Boston & Pittsburgh 1928 – 29 NHL
Boston Bruins 1929 – 30 NHL

	GP	G	A	PTS	PIM
RS†	388	246	19	265	79
PO†	50	19	0	19	6

MAHOVLICH, FRANK
Timmins, Ontario
1938 –
Inducted 1981

Toronto St. Michael's 1953 – 57 OHA
Toronto Maple Leafs 1956 – 68 NHL
Detroit Red Wings 1967 – 71 NHL
Montreal Canadiens 1970 – 74 NHL
Toronto Toros 1974 – 76 WHA
Birmingham Bulls 1976 – 78 WHA

	GP	G	A	PTS	PIM
RS	1181	533	570	1103	1056
PO	137	51	67	118	163

MALONE, "PHANTOM" JOE
Sillery, Quebec
1890 – 1969
Inducted 1950

Quebec Bulldogs 1908 – 09 ECHA
Waterloo 1909 – 10 OPHL
Quebec Bulldogs 1910 – 17 NHA
Montreal Canadiens 1917 – 19 &
1920 – 21 & 1922 – 24 NHL
Quebec Bulldogs 1919 – 20 NHL
Hamilton Tigers 1921 – 22 NHL

	GP	G	A	PTS	PIM
RS	125	146	18	164	35
PO	7	7	1	8	0

MANTHA, SYLVIO
Montreal, Quebec
1902 – 1974
Inducted 1960

Montreal Imperials 1920 – 23 ⸺
Montreal Canadiens 1923 – 36 NHL
Boston Bruins 1936 – 37 NHL

	GP	G	A	PTS	PIM
RS	543	63	72	135	667
PO	46	5	4	9	66

MARSHALL, JACK
St. Vallier, Quebec
1877 – 1965
Inducted 1965

Montreal Pointe Charles High School
1894 – 98
Winnipeg Victorias 1898 – 1901 MHL
Montreal Victorias 1901 – 03 CAHL
Montreal Wanderers 1903 – 05 FAHL
Montreal Montagnards 1905 – 06 FAHL
Montreal Wanderers 1906 – 07 ECAHA
Montreal Shamrocks 1907 – 08 ECAHA
Montreal Shamrocks 1908 – 09 ECHA
Montreal Wanderers 1909 – 12 NHA
Toronto Tecumsehs 1912 – 13 NHA
Toronto Ontarios 1913 – 14 NHA
Toronto Shamrocks 1914 – 15 NHA
Montreal Wanderers 1915 – 17 NHA

	GP	G	A	PTS	PIM
RS*	132	99	x	99	x
PO*	18	13	x	13	x

Players

MAXWELL, FRED
Winnipeg, Manitoba
1890 – 1975
Inducted 1962

Winnipeg Monarchs 1914 – 16 MSHL
Winnipeg Falcons 1918 – 25 MSHL

	GP	G	A	PTS	PIM
RS	x	x	x	x	x
PO	x	x	x	x	x

McDONALD, LANNY
Hanna, Alberta
1953 –
Inducted 1992

Medicine Hat Tigers 1971 – 73 WHL
Toronto Maple Leafs 1973 – 80 NHL
Colorado Rockies 1979 – 82 NHL
Calgary Flames 1981 – 89 NHL

	GP	G	A	PTS	PIM
RS	1111	500	506	1006	899
PO	117	44	40	84	120

McGEE, FRANK
Ottawa, Ontario
Born late 1800's – 1916
Inducted 1945

Ottawa Senators 1902 – 04 CAHL
Ottawa Senators 1904 – 05 FAHL
Ottawa Senators 1905 – 06 ECAHA

	GP	G	A	PTS	PIM
RS*	23	71	x	71	x
PO*	22	63	x	63	x

McGIMSIE, BILLY
Woodsville, Ontario
1880 – 1968
Inducted 1962

Rat Portage Thistles 1902 – 03 &
1904 – 06 MHSHA
Kenora Thistles 1906 – 07 MHL

	GP	G	A	PTS	PIM
RS*	x	x	x	x	x
PO*	7	4	x	4	x

McNAMARA, GEORGE
Penetang, Ontario
1886 – 1952
Inducted 1958

Montreal Shamrocks 1907 – 08 ECAHA
Montreal Shamrocks 1908 – 09 ECHA
Halifax Crescents 1909 – 12 MPL
Waterloo 1911 OPHL
Toronto Tecumsehs 1912 – 13 NHA
Ottawa/Ontario 1913 – 14 NHA
Toronto Shamrocks 1914 – 15 NHA
Toronto Blueshirts 1915 – 16 NHA
228th Battalion 1916 – 17 NHA

	GP	G	A	PTS	PIM
RS*	121	39	x	39	x
PO*	3	2	x	2	x

MIKITA, STAN
Skolce, Czechoslovakia
1940 –
Inducted 1983

St. Catharines Tee Pees 1956 – 59 OHA
Chicago Blackhawks 1958 – 80 NHL

	GP	G	A	PTS	PIM
RS	1394	541	926	1467	1270
PO	155	59	91	150	169

MOORE, DICKIE
Montreal, Quebec
1931 –
Inducted 1974

Montreal Royals 1949 – 51 QSHL
Montreal Canadiens 1951 – 63 NHL
Buffalo Bisons 1952 – 53 AHL
Montreal Royals 1953 – 54 QHL
Toronto Maple Leafs 1964 – 65 NHL
St. Louis Blues 1967 – 68 NHL

	GP	G	A	PTS	PIM
RS	719	261	347	608	652
PO	135	46	64	110	122

MORENZ, HOWIE
Mitchell, Ontario
1902 – 1937
Inducted 1945

Stratford Streak 1918 – 23 OHA
Montreal Canadiens 1923 – 34 &
1936 – 37 NHL
Chicago Blackhawks 1934 – 36 NHL
NY Rangers 1935 – 36 NHL

	GP	G	A	PTS	PIM
RS	550	270	197	467	531
PO	47	21	11	32	68

MOSIENKO, BILL
Winnipeg, Manitoba
1921 – 1994
Inducted 1965

Winnipeg Monarchs 1939 – 40 MJHL
Providence Reds 1940 – 41 AHL
Kansas City Americans 1940 – 42 AHA
Chicago Blackhawks 1941 – 55 NHL
Winnipeg Warriors 1955 – 59 WHL

	GP	G	A	PTS	PIM
RS	711	258	282	540	121
PO	22	10	4	14	15

NIGHBOR, FRANK
Pembroke, Ontario
1893 – 1966
Inducted 1947

Port Arthur Debaters 1907 – 11 ⸺
Port Arthur Hockey Club 1911 – 12 NOHA
Toronto Blueshirts 1912 – 13 NHA
Vancouver Millionaires 1913 – 15 PCHA
Ottawa Senators 1915 – 17 NHA
Ottawa Senators 1917 – 29 NHL
Toronto Maple Leafs 1929 – 30 NHL

	GP	G	A	PTS	PIM
RS	348	136	60	196	266
PO	36	11	10	21	27

NOBLE, REGINALD (REG)
Collingwood, Ontario
1895 – 1962
Inducted 1962

Canadiens/Toronto 1916 – 17 NHA
Toronto Arenas 1917 – 19 NHL
Toronto St. Patricks 1919 – 25 NHL
Montreal Maroons 1924 – 27 NHL
Detroit Cougars 1927 – 32 NHL
Detroit & Montreal 1932 – 33 NHL

	GP	G	A	PTS	PIM
RS†	534	180	79	259	770
PO†	34	4	5	9	39

O'CONNOR, BUDDY
Montreal, Quebec
1916 – 1977
Inducted 1988

Montreal Royals 1934 – 42 QSHL
Montreal Canadiens 1941 – 47 NHL
NY Rangers 1947 – 51 NHL
Cincinnati Mohawks 1951 – 52 AHL

	GP	G	A	PTS	PIM
RS	509	140	257	397	34
PO	53	15	21	36	6

OLIVER, HARRY
Selkirk, Manitoba
1898 – 1985
Inducted 1967

Selkirk Fishermen 1915 – 20 MHL
Calgary Canadians 1920 – 21 Big 4
Calgary Tigers 1921 – 25 WCHL
Calgary Tigers 1925 – 26 WHL
Boston Bruins 1926 – 34 NHL
NY Americans 1934 – 37 NHL

	GP	G	A	PTS	PIM
RS†	603	216	85	301	147
PO†	47	13	6	19	22

Players			Games Played	Goals	Assists	Total Points	Penalty Minutes
OLMSTEAD, BERT Scepter, Saskatchewan 1926 – Inducted 1985	Moosejaw Canucks 1944 – 46 SJHL Kansas City Play-Mors 1946 – 49 USHL Chicago Blackhawks 1948 – 51 NHL Milwaukee Seagulls 1950 – 51 USHL Montreal Canadiens 1950 – 58 NHL Toronto Maple Leafs 1958 – 62 NHL	RS PO	848 115	181 16	421 42	602 58	884 101
ORR, ROBERT (BOBBY) Parry Sound, Ontario 1948 – Inducted 1979	Oshawa Generals 1962 – 66 OHA Boston Bruins 1966 – 76 NHL Chicago Blackhawks 1976 – 79 NHL	RS PO	657 74	270 26	645 66	915 92	953 107
PARK, BRAD Toronto, Ontario 1948 – Inducted 1988	Toronto Marlboros 1965 – 68 OHA Buffalo Bisons 1968 – 69 AHL NY Rangers 1968 – 76 NHL Boston Bruins 1975 – 83 NHL Detroit Red Wings 1983 – 85 NHL	RS PO	1113 161	213 35	683 90	896 125	1429 217
PATRICK, LESTER Drummondville, Quebec 1883 – 1960 Inducted 1947	Brandon 1903 – 04 MHL Westmount 1904 – 05 CAHL Montreal Wanderers 1905 – 07 ECAHA Edmonton 1907 – 08 —— Nelson 1907 – 09 —— Ren. Cream. Kings 1909 – 10 NHA Victoria Aristocrats 1911 – 16 & 1918 – 22 PCHA Spokane Canaries 1916 – 17 PCHA Seattle Metros 1917 – 18 PCHA Victoria Cougars 1925 – 26 WHL NY Rangers 1927 – 28 NHL	RS* PO*	207 21	130 20	x x	130 20	x x
PATRICK, JOSEPH LYNN Victoria, British Columbia 1912 – 1980 Inducted 1980	Montreal Royals 1933 – 34 MHL NY Rangers 1934 – 43 & 1945 – 46 NHL Newhaven Ramblers 1946 – 47 AHL	RS PO	455 44	145 10	190 6	335 16	270 22
PERREAULT, GILBERT Victoriaville, Quebec 1950 – Inducted 1990	Montreal Canadiens 1967 – 70 OHA Buffalo Sabres 1970 – 87 NHL	RS PO	1191 90	512 33	814 70	1326 103	500 44
PHILLIPS, TOM Kenora, Ontario 1880 – 1923 Inducted 1945	Montreal AAA's 1902 – 03 CAHL Toronto Marlboros 1903 – 04 OHA Rat Portage Thistles 1904 – 06 MNSHA Kenora Thistles 1906 – 07 MHL Ottawa Senators 1907 – 08 ECAHA Vancouver Millionaires 1911 – 12 PCHA	RS* PO*	33 16	57 27	x x	57 27	x x
PILOTE, PIERRE Kenogami, Quebec 1931 – Inducted 1975	St. Catharines Tee Pees 1950 – 52 OHA Buffalo Bisons 1951 – 56 AHL Chicago Blackhawks 1955 – 68 NHL Toronto Maple Leafs 1968 – 69 NHL	RS PO	890 86	80 8	418 53	498 61	1251 102
PITRE, DIDIER "CANNONBALL" Valleyfield, Quebec 1883 – 1934 Inducted 1962	Montreal Nationals 1903 – 04 FAHL Montreal Nationals 1904 – 05 CAHL Montreal Shamrocks 1907 – 08 ECAHA Edmonton 1907 – 08 —— Renfrew Millionaires 1908 – 09 NHA Montreal Canadiens 1909 – 13 & 1914 – 17 NHA Vancouver Millionaires 1913 – 14 PCHA Montreal Canadiens 1917 – 23 NHL	RS† PO†	282 27	238 13	17 2	255 15	59 0
POTVIN, DENIS Ottawa, Ontario 1953 – Inducted 1991	Ottawa 67's 1968 – 73 OHA NY Islanders 1973 – 88 NHL	RS PO	1060 185	310 56	742 108	1052 164	1354 253
PRATT, WALTER "BABE" Stony Mountain, Manitoba 1916 – 1988 Inducted 1966	Kenora Thistles 1933 – 35 MJHL NY Rangers 1935 – 43 NHL Toronto Maple Leafs 1942 – 46 NHL Boston Bruins 1946 – 47 NHL	RS PO	517 63	83 12	209 17	292 29	453 90
PRIMEAU, JOE Lindsay, Ontario 1906 – 1989 Inducted 1963	Toronto Ravinas 1927 – 28 CPHL London Tecumsehs 1928 – 29 CPHL Toronto Maple Leafs 1927 – 36 NHL	RS PO	310 38	66 5	177 18	243 23	105 12
PRONOVOST, MARCEL Lac la Tortue, Quebec 1930 – Inducted 1978	Windsor Spitfires 1947 – 49 OHA Omaha Knights 1949 – 50 USHL Indianapolis Capitols 1950 – 51 AHL Detroit Red Wings 1949 – 65 NHL Toronto Maple Leafs 1965 – 70 NHL Tulsa 1969 – 71 CHL	RS PO	1206 134	88 8	257 23	345 31	851 104
PULFORD, BOB Newton Robinson, Ontario 1936 – Inducted 1991	Toronto Marlboros 1953 – 56 OHA Toronto Maple Leafs 1956 – 70 NHL LA Kings 1970 – 72 NHL	RS PO	1079 89	281 25	362 26	643 51	792 126
PULFORD, HARVEY Toronto, Ontario 1875 – 1940 Inducted 1945	Ottawa Senators 1893 – 98 AHA Ottawa Senators 1900 – 04 CAHL Ottawa Senators 1904 – 05 FAHL Ottawa Senators 1905 – 08 ECAHA	RS* PO*	96 22	6 2	x x	6 2	x x
QUACKENBUSH, BILL Toronto, Ontario 1922 – Inducted 1976	Indianapolis Capitols 1942 – 44 AHL Detroit Red Wings 1942 – 49 NHL Boston Bruins 1949 – 56 NHL	RS PO	774 79	62 2	222 19	284 21	95 8
RANKIN, FRANK Stratford, Ontario 1890 – 1932 Inducted 1961	Stratford 1906 – 09 OHA Eaton's Athletic Association 1910 – 12 OHA St. Michael's 1912 – 13 OHA	RS PO	x x	x x	x x	x x	x x
RATELLE, JEAN Lac St. Jean, Quebec 1940 – Inducted 1985	Guelph Biltmores 1958 – 60 OHA Trois Rivières Lions 1959 – 60 EPHL Kitchener-Waterloo Beavers 1961 – 62 EPHL NY Rangers 1962 – 76 NHL Baltimore Clippers 1962 – 65 AHL Boston Bruins 1975 – 81 NHL	RS PO	1281 123	491 32	776 66	1267 98	276 24
REARDON, KENNETH JOSEPH Winnipeg, Manitoba 1921 – Inducted 1966	Edmonton Athletic Club 1938 – 40 EJHL Montreal Canadiens 1940 – 42 & 1945 – 50 NHL Ottawa Commandos 1942 – 43 QSHL Montreal Canadiens 1945 – 46 QSHL	RS PO	341 31	26 2	96 5	122 7	604 62
RICHARD, HENRI Montreal, Quebec 1936 – Inducted 1979	Montreal Canadiens 1952 – 55 QJHL Montreal Canadiens 1955 – 75 NHL	RS PO	1256 180	358 49	688 80	1046 129	928 181
RICHARD, MAURICE "ROCKET" Montreal, Quebec 1921 – Inducted 1961	Verdun Maple Leafs 1938 – 40 QSHL Montreal Canadiens 1940 – 42 QSHL Montreal Canadiens 1942 – 60 NHL	RS PO	978 133	544 82	421 44	965 126	1285 188
RICHARDSON, GEORGE Kingston, Ontario 1887 – 1916 Inducted 1950	14th Regiment 1906 – 1912 Queen's University 1908 – 09	RS PO	x x	x x	x x	x x	x x
ROBERTS, GORDON Ottawa, Ontario 1891 – 1966 Inducted 1971	Ottawa Senators 1909 – 10 NHA Montreal Wanderers 1910 – 16 NHA Vancouver Millionaires 1916 – 17 & 1919 – 20 PCHA Seattle Metropolitans 1917 – 18 PCHA	RS* PO*	166 7	203 8	x x	x x	x x
ROBINSON, LARRY Winchester, Ontario 1951 – Inducted 1995	Metcalfe Jets 1967 – 68 JR. B Brockville Braves 1968 – 70 COJHL Kitchener Rangers 1970 – 71 OHA Nova Scotia Voyageurs 1971 – 74 AHL Montreal Canadiens 1972 – 89 NHL LA Kings 1989 – 92 NHL	RS PO	1384 227	208 28	750 116	958 144	793 211
ROSS, ART Naughton, Ontario 1886 – 1964 Inducted 1945	Montreal Westmount 1900 – 03 AHAC Westmount Academy 1902 – 05 CAHL Brandon 1906 – 07 MHL Kenora Thistles 1906 – 07 MHL Montreal Wanderers 1907 – 08 ECAHA Montreal Wanderers 1908 – 09 ECHA Haileybury Comets 1909 – 10 NHA Montreal Wanderers 1910 – 14 & 1916 – 17 NHA Ottawa Senators 1914 – 16 NHA Montreal Wanderers 1917 – 18 NHL	RS† PO†	167 16	85 6	0 0	85 6	0 0

Players

RUSSEL, BLAIR
Montreal, Quebec
1880 – 1961
Inducted 1965

Montreal Victorias 1894 – 99 AHAC
Montreal Victorias 1899 – 1905 CAHL
Montreal Victorias 1905 – 08 ECAHA

	Games Played	Goals	Assists	Total Points	Penalty Minutes
RS*	67	110	x	110	x
PO*	2	0	x	0	x

RUSSELL, ERNIE
Montreal, Quebec
1883 – 1963
Inducted 1965

Sterling 1902 – 04 AHAC
Montreal AAA's 1904 – 05 CAHL
Montreal Wanderers 1905 – 07 ECAHA
Montreal Wanderers 1907 – 08 & 1909 – 14 NHA

	Games Played	Goals	Assists	Total Points	Penalty Minutes
RS*	98	180	x	180	x
PO*	11	31	x	31	x

RUTTAN, JACK
Winnipeg, Manitoba
1889 – 1973
Inducted 1962

Armstrong's Point 1905 – 06
Rustler 1906 – 07
St. Johns College 1907 – 08
Manitoba Varsity 1909 – 12 WSHL
Winnipeg 1912 – 13 WpgHL

	Games Played	Goals	Assists	Total Points	Penalty Minutes
RS	x	x	x	x	x
PO	x	x	x	x	x

SAVARD, SERGE
Montreal, Quebec
1946 –
Inducted 1986

Montreal Canadiens 1963 – 66 OHA
Omaha Knights 1964 – 65 CPHL
Quebec Aces 1966 – 67 AHL
Houston Apollos 1966 – 67 CPHL
Montreal Canadiens 1966 – 81 NHL
Winnipeg Jets 1981 – 83 NHL

	Games Played	Goals	Assists	Total Points	Penalty Minutes
RS	1040	106	333	439	592
PO	130	19	49	68	88

SCANLAN, FRED
———
Inducted 1965

Montreal Shamrocks 1897 – 98 AHA
Montreal Shamrocks 1898 – 1901 CAHL
Winnipeg Victorias 1901 – 03 MHL

	Games Played	Goals	Assists	Total Points	Penalty Minutes
RS*	31	16	x	16	x
PO*	17	6	x	6	x

SCHMIDT, MILT
Kitchener, Ontario
1918 –
Inducted 1961

Kitchener Waterloo Greenshirts 1934 – 36 OHA
Providence Reds 1936 – 37 IAHL
Boston Bruins 1936 – 42 & 1945 – 55 NHL
RCAF Flyers 1942 – 45

	Games Played	Goals	Assists	Total Points	Penalty Minutes
RS	778	229	346	575	466
PO	86	24	25	49	60

SCHRINER, DAVID "SWEENEY"
Calgary, Alberta
1911 – 1990
Inducted 1962

Syracuse Stars 1933 – 34 IHL
NY Americans 1934 – 39 NHL
Toronto Maple Leafs 1939 – 43 & 1944 – 46 NHL

	Games Played	Goals	Assists	Total Points	Penalty Minutes
RS	484	201	204	405	148
PO	60	18	11	29	44

SEIBERT, EARL
Kitchener, Ontario
1911 – 1990
Inducted 1963

Springfield Indians 1929 – 31 CAHL
NY Rangers 1931 – 36 NHL
Chicago Blackhawks 1935 – 45 NHL
Detroit Red Wings 1944 – 46 NHL

	Games Played	Goals	Assists	Total Points	Penalty Minutes
RS	650	89	187	276	768
PO	66	11	8	19	76

SEIBERT, OLIVER
Berlin, Ontario
1881 – 1944
Inducted 1961

Berlin Dutchmen 1900 – 07 WOHA
Canadian Soo 1904 – 05 IHL

	Games Played	Goals	Assists	Total Points	Penalty Minutes
RS	x	x	x	x	x
PO	x	x	x	x	x

SHORE, EDDIE
Fort Qu'Appelle, Saskatchewan
1902 – 1985
Inducted 1947

Melville Millionaires 1923 – 24 SSHL
Regina Capitals 1924 – 25 WCHL
Edmonton Eskimo 1925 – 26 WHL
Boston Bruins 1926 – 40 NHL

	Games Played	Goals	Assists	Total Points	Penalty Minutes
RS	550	105	179	284	1037
PO	55	6	13	19	179

SHUTT, STEPHEN "STEVE"
Toronto, Ontario
1952 –
Inducted 1993

Toronto 1968 – 69 JR. A & B OHA
Toronto Marlboros 1969 – 72 JR. A OHA
Nova Scotia Voyageurs 1972 – 73 AHL
Montreal Canadiens 1973 – 85 NHL
Los Angeles Kings 1984 – 85 NHL

	Games Played	Goals	Assists	Total Points	Penalty Minutes
RS†	1122	582	527	1089	650
PO†	99	50	48	98	65

SIEBERT, ALBERT CHARLES "BABE"
Plattsville, Ontario
1904 – 1939
Inducted 1964

Niagara Falls 1924 – 25 OHA
Montreal Maroons 1925 – 32 NHL
NY Rangers 1932 – 34 NHL
Boston Bruins 1933 – 36 NHL
Montreal Canadiens 1936 – 39 NHL

	Games Played	Goals	Assists	Total Points	Penalty Minutes
RS	593	140	156	296	972
PO	54	8	7	15	62

SIMPSON, JOE
Selkirk, Manitoba
1893 – 1973
Inducted 1962

Selkirk Fishermen 1918 – 20 MHL
Edmonton Eskimos 1921 – 25 WCHL
NY Americans 1925 – 31 NHL

	Games Played	Goals	Assists	Total Points	Penalty Minutes
RS†	340	76	19	95	176
PO†	8	1	x	1	x

SITTLER, DARRYL
St. Jacobs, Ontario
1950 –
Inducted 1989

London Nationals/Knights 1967 – 70 OHA
Toronto Maple Leafs 1970 – 82 NHL
Philadelphia Flyers 1981 – 84 NHL
Detroit Red Wings 1984 – 85 NHL

	Games Played	Goals	Assists	Total Points	Penalty Minutes
RS	1096	484	637	1121	948
PO	76	29	45	74	137

SMITH, ALF
Ottawa, Ontario
1873 – 1953
Inducted 1962

Ottawa Senators 1894 – 97 AHA
Ottawa Senators 1903 – 04 CAHL
Ottawa Senators 1904 – 05 FAHL
Ottawa Senators 1905 – 08 ECAHA
Kenora Thistles 1906 – 07 MHL

	Games Played	Goals	Assists	Total Points	Penalty Minutes
RS*	65	90	x	90	x
PO*	22	36	x	36	x

SMITH, CLINT
Assiniboia, Saskatchewan
1913 –
Inducted 1991

Vancouver Lions 1933 – 36 NWHL
NY Rangers 1936 – 43 NHL
Chicago Blackhawks 1943 – 47 NHL

	Games Played	Goals	Assists	Total Points	Penalty Minutes
RS	483	161	236	397	24
PO	44	10	14	24	2

SMITH, REGINALD JOSEPH "HOOLEY"
Toronto, Ontario
1905 – 1963
Inducted 1972

Toronto Granites 1920 – 24 OHA
Ottawa Senators 1924 – 27 NHL
Montreal Maroons 1927 – 36 NHL
Boston Bruins 1936 – 37 NHL
NY Americans 1937 – 41 NHL

	Games Played	Goals	Assists	Total Points	Penalty Minutes
RS	715	200	215	415	1013
PO	54	11	8	19	109

SMITH, TOMMY
Ottawa, Ontario
1885 – 1966
Inducted 1973

Ottawa Victorias 1905 – 06 FAHL
Ottawa Senators 1905 – 06 ECAHA
Brantford Indians 1908 – 10 OPHL
Cobalt Silver Kings 1909 – 10 NHA
Galt 1910 – 11 OPHL
Moncton 1911 – 12 MPL
Quebec Bulldogs 1912 – 16 NHA
Ontarios 1914 – 15 NHA
Montreal Canadiens 1916 – 17 NHA
Quebec Bulldogs 1919 – 20 NHL

	Games Played	Goals	Assists	Total Points	Penalty Minutes
RS*	x	240	x	240	x
PO*	15	15	x	15	x

STANLEY, ALLAN
Timmins, Ontario
1926 –
Inducted 1981

Providence Reds 1946 – 49 AHL
NY Rangers 1948 – 55 NHL
Vancouver Canucks 1953 – 54 WHL
Chicago Blackhawks 1954 – 56 NHL
Boston Bruins 1956 – 58 NHL
Toronto Maple Leafs 1958 – 68 NHL
Philadelphia Flyers 1968 – 69 NHL

	Games Played	Goals	Assists	Total Points	Penalty Minutes
RS	1244	100	333	433	792
PO	109	7	36	43	80

STANLEY, BARNEY
Paisley, Ontario
1893 – 1971
Inducted 1962

Vancouver Millionaires 1914 – 19 PCHA
Calgary Tigers 1921 – 22 WCHL
Regina Capitals 1922 – 24 WCHL
Edmonton Eskimos 1924 – 25 WCHL
Edmonton Eskimos 1925 – 26 WHL

	Games Played	Goals	Assists	Total Points	Penalty Minutes
RS*	216	144	x	144	x
PO*	19	11	x	11	x

STEWART, JACK
Pilot Mound, Manitoba
1917 – 1983
Inducted 1964

Portage Terriers 1935 – 37 MJHL
Pittsburgh Hornets 1937 – 39 IAHL
Detroit Red Wings 1938 – 43 & 1945 – 50 NHL
Chicago Blackhawks 1950 – 52 NHL

	Games Played	Goals	Assists	Total Points	Penalty Minutes
RS	565	31	84	115	765
PO	80	5	14	19	143

STEWART, NELSON
Montreal, Quebec
1902 – 1957
Inducted 1962

Cleveland 1920 – 25 USAHA
Montreal Maroons 1925 – 32 NHL
Boston Bruins 1932 – 35 & 1936 – 37 NHL
NY Americans 1935 – 40 NHL

	Games Played	Goals	Assists	Total Points	Penalty Minutes
RS	651	324	191	515	943
PO	54	15	13	28	61

STUART, BRUCE
Ottawa, Ontario
1882 – 1961
Inducted 1961

Ottawa Senators 1898 – 1900 & 1901 – 02 CAHL
Quebec Bulldogs 1900 – 01 CAHL
Pittsburgh 1902 – 03 IHL
Calumet 1903 – 07 IHL
Montreal Wanderers 1907 – 08 ECAHA
Ottawa Senators 1908 – 09 ECHA
Ottawa Senators 1909 – 11 NHA

	Games Played	Goals	Assists	Total Points	Penalty Minutes
RS*	45	63	x	63	x
PO*	7	17	x	17	x

STUART, WILLIAM HODGSON "HOD"
Ottawa, Ontario
1879 – 1907
Inducted 1945

Ottawa Senators 1898 – 1900 CAHL
Quebec Bulldogs 1900 – 02 CAHL
Pittsburgh 1902 – 03 IHL
Portage Lakes 1903 – 04 IHL
Calumet 1904 – 06 IHL
Montreal Wanderers 1906 – 07 ECAHA

	Games Played	Goals	Assists	Total Points	Penalty Minutes
RS*	33	16	x	16	x
PO*	4	0	x	0	x

TAYLOR, FREDERICK "CYCLONE"
Tara, Ontario
1883 – 1979
Inducted 1947

Listowel 1903 – 05 OHA
Portage Lakes 1905 – 07 IHL
Ottawa Senators 1907 – 09 ECAHA
Ren. Cream. Kings 1909 – 11 NHA
Vancouver Millionaires 1912 – 21 & 1922 – 23 PCHA

	Games Played	Goals	Assists	Total Points	Penalty Minutes
RS*	186	194	x	194	x
PO*	19	15	x	15	x

TRIHEY, HARRY
Montreal, Quebec
1877 – 1942
Inducted 1950

Montreal Ste. Marie College 1893 – 96
Montreal Shamrocks 1896 – 98 AHC
Montreal Shamrocks 1898 – 1901 CAHL

	Games Played	Goals	Assists	Total Points	Penalty Minutes
RS*	30	46	x	46	x
PO*	8	16	x	16	x

Players

			Games Played	Goals	Assists	Total Points	Penalty Minutes
ULLMAN, NORM Provost, Alberta 1935 – Inducted 1982	Edmonton Oil Kings 1951 – 54 WCJHL Edmonton Flyers 1953 – 55 WHL Detroit Red Wings 1955 – 68 NHL Toronto Maple Leafs 1967 – 75 NHL Edmonton Oilers 1975 – 77 WHA	RS PO	1410 106	490 30	739 53	1229 83	712 67
WALKER, JACK Silver Mountain, Ontario 1888 – 1950 Inducted 1960	Port Arthur Lake Cities 1910 – 11 NOHL Toronto Blueshirts 1912 – 15 NHA Seattle Metros 1915 – 24 PCHA Victoria Cougars 1924 – 25 WCHL Victoria Cougars 1925 – 26 WHL Detroit Cougars 1926 – 28 NHL	RS† PO†	361 46	135 20	8 x	143 20	18 x
WALSH, MARTY Kingston, Ontario 1883 – 1915 Inducted 1962	Queen's University 1902 – 06 Canada 500 1906 – 07 IHL Ottawa Senators 1907 – 08 ECAHA Ottawa Senators 1908 – 09 ECAHA Ottawa Senators 1909 – 12 NHA	RS* PO*	59 8	135 25	x x	135 25	x x
WATSON, HARRY Saskatoon, Saskatchewan 1923 – Inducted 1994	Saskatoon Chiefs 1938 – 39 Juvenile Saskatoon Dodgers 1939 – 40 SHL Saskatoon Quakers 1940 – 41 SHL Brooklyn Americans 1941 – 42 NHL Detroit Red Wings 1942 – 43 & 1945 – 46 NHL Montreal RCAF 1943 – 44 SR. QSHL Saskatoon Quakers 1943 – 44 SSHL Winnipeg RCAF 1943 – 44 SR. WMHL Toronto Maple Leafs 1946 – 55 NHL Chicago Blackhawks 1954 – 57 NHL Buffalo Bisons 1957 – 58 AHL	RS† PO†	877 68	280 26	246 10	506 36	172 29
WATSON, HARRY "MOOSE" St John's, Newfoundland 1898 – 1957 Inducted 1962	Aura Lee Juniors 1914 – 18 OHA St. Andrews 1915 OHA Toronto Dentals 1919 OHA Toronto Granites 1920 – 25 OHL Toronto Sea Fleas 1931 OHA	RS PO	x x	x x	x x	x x	x x
WEILAND, RALPH C. "COONEY" Seaforth, Ontario 1904 – 1985 Inducted 1971	Minneapolis Millers 1925 – 28 AHA Boston Bruins 1928 – 32 & 1935 – 39 NHL Ottawa Senators 1932 – 34 NHL Detroit Red Wings 1933 – 35 NHL	RS PO	509 45	173 12	160 10	333 22	147 12
WESTWICK, HARRY Ottawa, Ontario 1876 – 1957 Inducted 1962	Aberdeens 1894 – 98 AHA Ottawa Senators 1900 – 04 CAHL Ottawa Senators 1904 – 05 FAHL Ottawa Senators 1905 – 08 ECAHA Kenora Thistles 1906 – 07 MHL	RS* PO*	87 24	87 26	x x	87 26	x x
WHITCROFT, FRED Port Perry, Ontario 1882 – 1931 Inducted 1962	Kenora Thistles 1906 – 07 MHL Edmonton 1907 – 11 SR. Ren. Cream. Kings 1909 – 10 NHA	RS* PO*	9 8	55 14	x x	5 14	x x
WILSON, GORDON ALLAN "PHAT" Port Arthur, Ontario 1895 – 1970 Inducted 1962	Port Arthur War Veterans 1918 – 20 OHA Iroquois Falls Eskimos 1921 NOHA Port Arthur Bearcats 1923 – 33 OHA	RS PO	x x	x x	x x	x x	x x

Goalies

			Games Played	Minutes	Goals Against	Shutouts	Average
BENEDICT, CLINT Ottawa, Ontario 1891 – 1976 Inducted 1965	Ottawa New Edinburgh 1910 – 13 OCHL Ottawa Senators 1912 – 17 NHA Ottawa Senators 1917 – 24 NHL Montreal Maroons 1924 – 30 NHL	RS PO	362 48	22321 2907	863 87	57 15	2.32 1.80
BOWER, JOHNNY Prince Albert, Saskatchewan 1924 – Inducted 1976	Prince Albert Black Hawks 1944 – 45 SJHL Cleveland Barons 1945 – 53 & 1957 – 58 AHL Providence Reds 1945 – 46 & 1955 – 57 AHL NY Rangers 1953 – 55 & 56 – 57 NHL Vancouver Canucks 1954 – 55 WHL Toronto Maple Leafs 1958 – 70 NHL	RS PO	552 74	32077 4350	1347 184	37 5	2.52 2.54
BRIMSEK, FRANK Eveleth, Minnesota 1915 – Inducted 1966	Providence Reds 1937 – 39 IAHL Boston Bruins 1938 – 43 & 1945 – 49 NHL Chicago Blackhawks 1949 – 50 NHL	RS PO	514 68	31210 4365	1404 186	40 2	2.70 2.56

Goalies

			Games Played	Minutes	Goals Against	Shutouts	Average
BRODA, WALTER "TURK" Brandon, Manitoba 1914 – 1972 Inducted 1967	Winnipeg Monarchs 1933 – 35 MHL Detroit Olympics 1935 – 36 IHL Toronto Maple Leafs 1936 – 43 & 1945 – 52 NHL	RS PO	629 102	38167 6406	1609 211	62 13	2.53 1.98
CHEEVERS, GERRY St. Catharines, Ontario 1940 – Inducted 1985	Toronto St. Michael's 1956 – 61 OHA Toronto Maple Leafs 1961 – 62 NHL Sault Ste. Marie Thunderbirds 1961 – 62 CPHL Pittsburgh Hornets 1961 – 62 AHL Rochester Americans 1961 – 65 AHL Sudbury Wolves 1962 – 63 EPHL Boston Bruins 1965 – 72 & 1975 – 80 NHL Oklahoma City Blazers 1965 – 67 CPHL Cleveland Crusaders 1972 – 76 WHA	RS PO	418 88	24394 5396	1175 242	26 8	2.89 2.69
CONNELL, ALEX Ottawa, Ontario 1902 – 1958 Inducted 1958	Ottawa Shamrocks 1920 – 24 OCHL Ottawa Senators 1924 – 31 & 1932 – 33 NHL Detroit Falcons 1931 – 32 NHL NY Americans 1933 – 34 NHL Montreal Maroons 1934 – 35 & 1936 – 37 NHL	RS PO	417 21	26030 1309	830 26	81 4	1.91 1.19
DRYDEN, KEN Hamilton, Ontario 1947 – Inducted 1983	Cornell University 1969 – 70 Montreal Voyageurs 1970 – 71 AHL Montreal Canadiens 1970 – 73 & 1974 – 79 NHL	RS PO	397 112	23352 6846	870 274	46 10	2.24 2.40
DURNAN, BILL Toronto, Ontario 1916 – 1972 Inducted 1964	Lakeshore Blue Devils 1936 – 40 NOHA Montreal Royals 1940 – 43 QSHL Montreal Canadiens 1943 – 50 NHL	RS PO	383 45	22945 2851	901 99	34 2	2.36 2.08
ESPOSITO, TONY Sault Ste. Marie, Ontario 1943 – Inducted 1988	Michigan Tech 1963 – 67 Vancouver Canucks 1967 – 68 WHL Montreal Canadiens 1968 – 69 NHL Houston Apollos 1968 – 69 CHL Chicago Blackhawks 1969 – 84 NHL	RS PO	886 99	52585 6017	2563 308	76 6	2.92 3.07
GARDINER, CHUCK Edinburgh, Scotland 1904 – 1934 Inducted 1945	Selkirk Fishermen 1924 – 25 MHL Winnipeg Maroons 1925 – 27 AHA Chicago Blackhawks 1927 – 34 NHL	RS PO	316 21	19687 1532	664 35	42 5	2.05 1.37
GIACOMIN, EDDIE Sudbury, Ontario 1939 – Inducted 1987	Bell Telephone 1958 – 59 IND. Providence Reds 1959 – 65 AHL New York Rovers 1960 – 62 EHL Baltimore Clippers 1965 – 66 AHL NY Rangers 1965 – 76 NHL Detroit Red Wings 1975 – 78 NHL	RS PO	610 65	35693 3834	1675 180	54 1	2.82 2.82
HAINSWORTH, GEORGE Toronto, Ontario 1895 – 1950 Inducted 1961	Kitchener Greenshirts 1917 – 23 OHA Saskatoon Crescents 1923 – 25 WCHL Saskatoon Crescents 1925 – 26 WHL Montreal Canadiens 1926 – 33 & 1936 – 37 NHL Toronto Maple Leafs 1933 – 37 NHL	RS PO	465 52	29415 3486	937 112	94 8	1.91 1.93
HALL, GLENN Humboldt, Saskatchewan 1931 – Inducted 1975	Windsor Spitfires 1949 – 51 OHA Indianapolis Capitols 1951 – 52 AHL Detroit Red Wings 1952 – 53 & 1954 – 57 NHL Edmonton Flyers 1952 – 55 WHL Chicago Blackhawks 1957 – 67 NHL St. Louis Blues 1967 – 71 NHL	RS PO	906 115	53464 6899	2239 321	84 6	2.51 2.79
HERN, RILEY St. Mary's, Ontario 1880 – 1929 Inducted 1962	Portage Lakes 1903 – 06 IHL Montreal Wanderers 1906 – 08 ECAHA Montreal Wanderers 1908 – 09 ECHA Montreal Wanderers 1909 – 11 NHA	RS* PO*	60 14	x x	281 54	1 0	4.68 3.86
HOLMES, HARRY "HAP" Aurora, Ontario 1889 – 1940 Inducted 1972	Toronto Parkdales 1910 – 12 OHA Toronto Blueshirts 1912 – 16 NHA Seattle Metros 1915 – 17 & 1918 – 24 PCHA Toronto Arenas 1917 – 19 NHL Victoria Aristocrats 1924 – 25 WCHL Victoria Aristocrats 1925 – 26 WHL Detroit Cougars 1926 – 28 NHL	RS† PO†	410 52	6510 420	1191 126	41 6	2.90 2.42

Goalies

			Games Played	Minutes	Goals Against	Shutouts	Average
HUTTON, BOUSE Ottawa, Ontario 1877 – 1962 Inducted 1962	Ottawa Senators 1898 – 1904 CAHL Ottawa Senators 1908 – 09 FAHL	RS*	36	x	106	2	2.94
		PO*	12	x	28	2	2.33
LEHMAN, HUGH Pembroke, Ontario 1885 – 1961 Inducted 1958	Pembroke 1906 – 08 UOVHL Berlin Dutchmen 1908 – 1911 OPHL New Westminster Royals 1911 – 14 PCHA Vancouver Millionaires 1914 – 26 PCHA Chicago Blackhawks 1926 – 28 NHL	RS†	403	3047	1451	23	3.60
		PO†	48	120	137	7	2.85
LeSUEUR, PERCY Quebec City, Quebec 1882 – 1962 Inducted 1961	Smith Falls 1905 – 06 FAHL Ottawa Senators 1905 – 08 ECAHA Ottawa Senators 1908 – 09 ECHA Ottawa Senators 1909 – 14 NHA Toronto Shamrocks 1914 – 15 NHA Toronto Blueshirts 1915 – 16 NHA	RS†	156	x	718	4	4.60
		PO†	9	x	40	0	4.44
LUMLEY, HARRY Owen Sound, Ontario 1926 – Inducted 1980	Barrie Colts 1942 – 43 OHA Indianapolis Capitols 1943 – 44 AHL Detroit Red Wings 1943 – 50 NHL Chicago Blackhawks 1950 – 52 NHL Toronto Maple Leafs 1952 – 56 NHL Boston Bruins 1957 – 60 NHL	RS	804	48097	2210	71	2.76
		PO	76	4778	199	7	2.50
MORAN, PADDY Quebec City, Quebec 1877 – 1966 Inducted 1958	Quebec 1899 – 1905 CAHL Quebec Bulldogs 1905 – 08 ECAHA Quebec Bulldogs 1908 – 09 ECHA Haileybury Comets 1909 – 10 NHA Quebec Bulldogs 1910 – 17 NHA	RS†	201	x	1094	2	5.44
		PO†	7	x	24	1	3.43
PARENT, BERNIE Montreal, Quebec 1945 – Inducted 1984	Niagara Falls Flyers 1963 – 65 OHA Oklahoma City Blazers 1965 – 67 CPHL Boston Bruins 1965 – 67 NHL Philadelphia Flyers 1967 – 71 & 1973 – 79 NHL Toronto Maple Leafs 1970 – 72 NHL Philadelphia Blazers 1972 – 73 WHA	RS	608	35136	1493	55	2.55
		PO	71	4302	174	6	2.43
PLANTE, JACQUES Shawinigan Falls, Quebec 1929 – 1986 Inducted 1978	Montreal Royals 1951 – 53 QSHL Buffalo Bisons 1952 – 54 AHL Montreal Canadiens 1952 – 63 NHL Montreal Royals 1960 – 61 EPHL NY Rangers 1963 – 65 NHL Baltimore Clippers 1964 – 65 AHL St. Louis Blues 1968 – 70 NHL Toronto Maple Leafs 1970 – 73 NHL Boston Bruins 1972 – 73 NHL Edmonton Oilers 1974 – 75 WHA	RS	837	49533	1965	82	2.38
		PO	112	6651	241	15	2.17
RAYNER, CHUCK Sutherland, Saskatchewan 1920 – Inducted 1973	Kenora Thistles 1937 – 40 MJHL Springfield 1940 – 42 AHL NY Americans 1940 – 41 NHL Brooklyn Americans 1941 – 42 NHL NY Rangers 1945 – 53 NHL	RS	425	25491	1295	25	3.05
		PO	18	1134	46	1	2.43
SAWCHUK, TERRY Winnipeg, Manitoba 1929 – 1970 Inducted 1971	Galt Red Wings 1946 – 47 OHA Omaha Knights 1947 – 48 USHL Indianapolis Capitols 1948 – 50 AHL Detroit Red Wings 1949 – 55 & 1957 – 64 & 1968 – 69 NHL Boston Bruins 1955 – 57 NHL Toronto Maple Leafs 1964 – 67 NHL LA Kings 1967 – 68 NHL NY Rangers 1969 – 70 NHL	RS	971	57114	2401	103	2.52
		PO	106	6311	267	12	2.54
SMITH, WILLIAM "BILL" Perth, Ontario 1950 – Inducted 1993	Cornwall Royals 1969 – 70 QJHL Springfield 1970 – 71 AHL Los Angeles Kings 1971 – 72 NHL New York Islanders 1972 – 89 NHL	RS†	813	46134	2519	29	3.16
		PO†	152	8869	414	7	2.73
THOMPSON, CECIL R. "TINY" Sandon, British Columbia 1905 – 1981 Inducted 1959	Minneapolis Millers 1925 – 28 AHA Boston Bruins 1928 – 39 NHL Detroit Red Wings 1939 – 40 NHL	RS	553	34174	1183	81	2.08
		PO	44	2970	93	7	1.88

Goalies

			Games Played	Minutes	Goals Against	Shutouts	Average
TRETIAK, VLADISLAV Moscow, USSR 1952 – Inducted 1989	Central Red Army 1969 – 84 Soviet National Team 1969 – 84	RS	x	x	x	x	x
		PO	x	x	x	x	x
VEZINA, GEORGES Chicoutimi, Quebec 1887 – 1926 Inducted 1945	Chicoutimi Senior 1905 – 10 Montreal Canadiens 1910 – 17 NHA Montreal Canadiens 1917 – 26 NHL	RS†	328	11564	1145	15	3.49
		PO†	38	1596	122	4	3.21
WORSLEY, LORNE "GUMP" Montreal, Quebec 1929 – Inducted 1980	Verdun 1946 – 49 QJHL New Haven Ramblers 1949 – 50 AHL St. Paul Saints 1950 – 51 USHL Saskatoon Quakers 1951 – 53 WHL Vancouver Canucks 1953 – 54 WHL NY Rangers 1952 – 63 NHL Providence Reds 1957 – 58 AHL Springfield Indians 1959 – 60 AHL Quebec Aces 1963 – 65 AHL Montreal Canadiens 1963 – 70 NHL Minnesota North Stars 1969 – 74 NHL	RS	862	50232	2432	43	2.90
		PO	70	4080	192	5	2.82
WORTERS, ROY Toronto, Ontario 1900 – 1957 Inducted 1969	Pittsburgh Yellow Jackets 1923 – 25 USAHA Pittsburgh Pirates 1925 – 28 NHL NY Americans 1928 – 37 NHL Montreal Maroons 1929 – 30 NHL	RS	484	30175	1143	66	2.27
		PO	11	690	24	3	2.09

Officials

ARMSTRONG, NEIL
Plympton Township, Ontario
1932 –
Inducted 1991

ASHLEY, JOHN
Galt, Ontario
1930 –
Inducted 1981

CHADWICK, BILL
New York City, New York
1915 –
Inducted 1964

D'AMICO, JOHN
Toronto, Ontario
1937 –
Inducted 1993

ELLIOTT, CHAUCER
Kingston, Ontario
1879 – 1913
Inducted 1961

HAYES, GEORGE
Montreal, Quebec
1914 – 1987
Inducted 1988

HEWITSON, BOBBY
Toronto, Ontario
1892 – 1969
Inducted 1963

ION, MICKEY
Paris, Ontario
1886 – 1964
Inducted 1961

PAVELICH, MATT
Park Hill Gold Mines, Ontario
1934 –
Inducted 1987

RODDEN, MIKE
Mattawa, Ontario
1891 – 1978
Inducted 1962

SMEATON, COOPER
Carleton Place, Ontario
1890 – 1978
Inducted 1961

STOREY, RED
Barrie, Ontario
1918 –
Inducted 1967

UDVARI, FRANK
Yugoslavia
1924 –
Inducted 1973

Builders

ADAMS, CHARLES
Newport, Vermont
1876 – 1947
Inducted 1960

ADAMS, WESTON
Springfield, Massachusetts
1904 – 1973
Inducted 1972

AHEARN, FRANK
Ottawa, Ontario
1886 – 1962
Inducted 1962

AHEARNE, BUNNY
County Wexford, Ireland
1900 – 1985
Inducted 1977

ALLAN, SIR MONTAGU
Montreal, Quebec
1860 – 1951
Inducted 1945

ALLEN, KEITH
Saskatoon, Saskatchewan
1923 –
Inducted 1992

BALLARD, HAROLD
Toronto, Ontario
1903 – 1990
Inducted 1977

BAUER, FATHER DAVID
Kitchener – Waterloo, Ontario
1924 – 1988
Inducted 1989

BICKELL, J.P.
Toronto, Ontario
1884 – 1951
Inducted 1978

BOWMAN, SCOTTY
Montreal, Quebec
1933 –
Inducted 1991

BROWN, GEORGE
Boston, Massachusetts
1880 – 1937
Inducted 1961

BROWN, WALTER
Boston, Massachusetts
1905 – 1964
Inducted 1962

BUCKLAND, FRANK
Gravenhurst, Ontario
1902 – 1991
Inducted 1975

BUTTERFIELD, JACK
Regina, Saskatchewan
1919 –
Inducted 1980

CALDER, FRANK
Bristol, England
1877 – 1943
Inducted 1947

Builders

CAMPBELL, ANGUS
Stayner, Ontario
1884 – 1976
Inducted 1964

CAMPBELL, CLARENCE
Fleming, Saskatchewan
1905 – 1984
Inducted 1966

CATTARINICH, JOSEPH
Levis, Quebec
1881 – 1938
Inducted 1977

DANDURAND, LÉO
Bourbonnais, Illinois
1889 – 1964
Inducted 1963

DILIO, FRANK
Montreal, Quebec
1912 –
Inducted 1964

DUDLEY, GEORGE
Midland, Ontario
1894 – 1960
Inducted 1958

DUNN, JAMES
Winnipeg, Manitoba
1898 – 1979
Inducted 1968

EAGLESON, ALAN
St. Catharines, Ontario
1933 –
Inducted 1989

FRANCIS, EMILE "THE CAT"
North Battleford, Saskatchewan
1926 –
Inducted 1982

GIBSON, JACK
Berlin (Kitchener), Ontario
1880 – 1955
Inducted 1976

GORMAN, TOMMY
Ottawa, Ontario
1886 – 1961
Inducted 1963

GRIFFITHS, FRANK
Burnaby, B.C.
1916 – 1994
Inducted 1993

HANLEY, BILL
Balleyeast, County of Antrim,
Northern Ireland
1915 – 1990
Inducted 1986

HAY, CHARLES
Kingston, Ontario
1902 – 1973
Inducted 1974

HENDY, JIM
Barbados, British West Indies
1905 – 1961
Inducted 1968

HEWITT, FOSTER
Toronto, Ontario
1902 – 1985
Inducted 1965

HEWITT, WILLIAM
Cobourg, Ontario
1875 – 1966
Inducted 1947

HUME, FRED
New Westminster,
British Columbia
1892 – 1967
Inducted 1962

IMLACH, GEORGE "PUNCH"
Toronto, Ontario
1918 – 1987
Inducted 1984

IVAN, TOMMY
Toronto, Ontario
1911 –
Inducted 1974

JENNINGS, WILLIAM
New York City, New York
1920 – 1981
Inducted 1975

JOHNSON, BOB
Minneapolis, Minnesota
1931 – 1991
Inducted 1992

JUCKES, GORDON
Watrous, Saskatchewan
1914 – 1994
Inducted 1979

KILPATRICK, JOHN
New York, NY
1889 – 1960
Inducted 1960

KNOX III, SEYMOUR
Buffalo, NY
1926 – 1996
Inducted 1993

LEADER, AL
Barnsley, Manitoba
1903 – 1982
Inducted 1969

LeBEL, ROBERT
Quebec City, Quebec
1905 –
Inducted 1970

LOCKHART, THOMAS
New York City, New York
1892 – 1979
Inducted 1965

LOICQ, PAUL
Brussels, Belgium
1890 – 1947
Inducted 1961

MARIUCCI, JOHN
Eveleth, Minnesota
1916 – 1987
Inducted 1985

MATHERS, FRANK
Winnipeg, Manitoba
1924 –
Inducted 1992

McLAUGHLIN, FREDERIC
Chicago, Illinois
1877 – 1944
Inducted 1963

MILFORD, JAKE
Charlottetown,
Prince Edward Island
1914 – 1984
Inducted 1984

MOLSON, SEN. HARTLAND
Montreal, Quebec
1907 –
Inducted 1973

NELSON, FRANCIS
————
Died 1932
Inducted 1947

NORRIS, BRUCE
Chicago, Illinois
1924 – 1986
Inducted 1969

NORRIS, JAMES
Chicago, Illinois
1906 – 1966
Inducted 1962

NORRIS SR., JAMES
St. Catharines, Ontario
1879 – 1952
Inducted 1958

NORTHEY, WILLIAM
Leeds, Quebec
1872 – 1963
Inducted 1947

O'BRIEN, JOHN AMBROSE
Renfrew, Ontario
1885 – 1968
Inducted 1962

O'NEILL, BRIAN
Montreal, Quebec
1929 –
Inducted 1994

PAGE, FREDERICK
Port Arthur, Ontario
1915 –
Inducted 1993

PATRICK, FRANK
Ottawa, Ontario
1885 – 1960
Inducted 1958

PICKARD, ALLAN
Exeter, Ontario
1895 – 1975
Inducted 1958

PILOUS, RUDY
Winnipeg, Manitoba
1914 – 1994
Inducted 1985

POILE, BUD
Fort William, Ontario
1924 –
Inducted 1990

POLLOCK, SAM
Montreal, Quebec
1925 –
Inducted 1978

RAYMOND, SEN. DONAT
————
1880 – 1963
Inducted 1958

ROBERTSON, JOHN ROSS
————
1841 – 1918
Inducted 1947

ROBINSON, CLAUDE
Harriston, Ontario
1881 – 1976
Inducted 1947

ROSS, PHILLIP
Montreal, Quebec
1858 – 1949
Inducted 1976

SABETZKI, DR. GUNTHER
Dusseldorf, Germany
1915 –
Inducted 1995

SELKE, FRANK
Kitchener, Ontario
1893 – 1985
Inducted 1960

SINDEN, HARRY
Collins Bay, Ontario
1932 –
Inducted 1983

SMITH, FRANK
Chatham, Ontario
1894 – 1964
Inducted 1962

SMYTHE, CONN
Toronto, Ontario
1895 – 1980
Inducted 1958

SNIDER, ED
Washington,
District of Columbia
1933 –
Inducted 1988

STANLEY, LORD (OF PRESTON)
London, England
1841 – 1908
Inducted 1945

STRACHAN, AL
Blackpool, England
1946 –
Inducted 1993

SUTHERLAND, CAPT. JOHN T.
Kingston, Ontario
1870 – 1955
Inducted 1947

TARASOV, ANATOLI
Moscow, Soviet Union
1918 – 1995
Inducted 1974

TORREY, BILL
Montreal, Quebec
1934 –
Inducted 1995

TURNER, LLOYD
Elmvale, Ontario
1884 – 1976
Inducted 1958

TUTT, WILLIAM THAYER
Coronado, California
1912 – 1989
Inducted 1978

VOSS, CARL
Cheslea, Massachusetts
1907 – 1993
Inducted 1974

WAGHORNE, FRED
Tunbridge Wells, England
1866 – 1956
Inducted 1961

WIRTZ, ARTHUR
Chicago, Illinois
1901 – 1983
Inducted 1971

WIRTZ, BILL
Detroit, Michigan
1929 –
Inducted 1976

ZIEGLER, JR., JOHN A.
Grosse Pointe, Michigan
1934 –
Inducted 1987

Media

ELMER FERGUSON MEMORIAL AWARD WINNERS
Selected by the professional Hockey Writers' Association in recognition of distinguished members of the newspaper profession whose words have brought honour to journalism and to hockey.

BARTON, CHARLIE
Buffalo-Courier Express 1985

BEAUCHAMP, JACQUES
*Montreal Matin/
Journal de Montreal* 1984

BRENNAN, BILL
Detroit News 1987

BURCHARD, JIM
New York World Telegram 1984

BURNETT, RED
Toronto Star 1984

CARROLL, AUSTIN "DINK"
Montreal Gazette 1984

COLEMAN, JIM
Southam Newspapers 1984

DAMATA, TED
Chicago Tribune 1984

DELANO, HUGH
New York Post 1991

DESJARDIN, MARCEL
Montreal La Presse 1984

DULMAGE, JACK
Windsor Star 1984

DUNNELL, MILT
Toronto Star 1984

FERGUSON, ELMER
Montreal Herald/Star 1984

FISHER, RED
Montreal Star/Gazette 1985

FITZGERALD, TOM
Boston Globe 1984

FRAYNE, TRENT
*Toronto Telegram/
Globe and Mail/
Toronto Sun* 1984

GATECLIFF, JACK
St. Catharines Standard 1995

GROSS, GEORGE
*Toronto Telegram/
Toronto Sun* 1985

JOHNSTON, DICK
Buffalo News 1986

LANEY, AL
New York Herald-Tribune 1984

LAROCHELLE, CLAUDE
Le Soleil 1989

L'ESPÉRANCE, ZOTIQUE
*le Journal de Montréal/
le Petit Journal* 1985

MAYER, CHARLES
*le Journal de Montréal/
La Patrie* 1985

MacLEOD, REX
*Globe and Mail/
Toronto Star* 1987

MONOHAN, LEO
*Boston Daily Record/
Record-American/
Herald American* 1985

MORIARTY, TIM
UPI/*Newsday* 1986

NICHOLS, JOE
New York Times 1984

O'BRIEN, ANDY
Weekend Magazine 1985

ORR, FRANK
Toronto Star 1989

OLAN, BEN
New York Associated Press 1987

O'MEARA, BASIL
Montreal Star 1984

PROUDFOOT, JIM
Toronto Star 1988

RAYMOND, BERTRAND
le Journal de Montréal 1990

ROSA, FRAN
Boston Globe 1987

STRACHAN, AL
*Globe and Mail/
Toronto Sun* 1993

VIPOND, JIM
Globe and Mail 1984

WALTER, LEWIS
Detroit Times 1984

YOUNG, SCOTT
Globe and Mail/Telegram 1988

FOSTER HEWITT MEMORIAL AWARD WINNERS
Selected by the NHL Broadcasters' Association in recognition of members of the radio and television industry who made outstanding contributions to their profession and the game during their career in hockey broadcasting.

CUSICK, FRED
Boston 1984

DARLING, EDGAR LEE "TED"
Buffalo 1994

GALLIVAN, DANNY
Montreal 1984

HEWITT, FOSTER
Toronto 1984

IRVIN JR., DICK
Montreal 1988

KELLY, DAN
St. Louis 1989

LECAVELLIER, RENÉ
Montreal 1984

LYNCH, BUDD
Detroit 1985

MARTYN, BRUCE
Detroit 1991

McDONALD, KEN "JIGGS"
Los Angeles, Atlanta,
NY Islanders 1990

McFARLANE, BRIAN
Hockey Night in Canada 1995

McKNIGHT, WES
Toronto 1986

PETTIT, LLOYD
Chicago 1986

ROBSON, JIM
Vancouver 1992

SHAVER, AL
Minnesota 1993

SMITH, DOUG
Montreal 1985

WILSON, BOB
Boston 1987

Index

Acknowledgements

CREATED AND PRODUCED BY OPUS PRODUCTIONS INC.

President/Creative Director: Derik Murray
Vice President, Production: David Counsell
Design Director: Don Bull
Creative Consultant/Photo Editor: Brian Daisley
Electronic Art: Joseph Llamzon, Guylaine Rondeau
Head Archival Visual Researcher: Andrew Bergant
Visual Research Coordinator: Colette Aubin
Visual Coordinator: Joanne Powers
Staff Photographer: Alastair Bird

Chief Financial Officer: Jamie Engen
General Counsel/Photo Permissions: Ruth Chang
Marketing Manager: David Attard
Sales Representative: Chris Richardson
Office Manager: Catherine Palmer

Vice President/Publishing Director: Marthe Love
Senior Editor: Brian Scrivener
Executive Publishing Coordinator: Wendy Darling
Publishing Associate: Jennifer Love
Editorial Coordinator: Michelle Hunter
Publicity Coordinator: Gillian Hurtig
Publishing Assistants: Iris Ho, Allie Wilmink
Proofreader/Indexer: Catherine Bennett
Reception: Azra Dias

Editorial Consultant: Sean Rossiter

Archival Researcher: Ronaldo Bayaton
Research Assistant: Rey Sandre
Print Archivist: Beth Brooks

Opus Productions would like to
thank the following:
Hockey Hall of Fame: Scotty Morrison, Jeffrey
D. Denomme, Bryan Black, Christine Simpson,
Philip Pritchard, Craig Campbell, Jeff Davis,
Scott North, Ray Paquet, Barry Eversley,
Janice McCabe, Sylvia Lau, Marilyn Robbins,
Pearl Rajwanth, Jane Rodney, Tom Gaston

Penguin Books Canada Ltd.: Steve Parr,
Brad Martin, Cynthia Good, Dianne Craig, Scott
Sellers, Barb Woodburne, Louise Curtis,
Kevin Gorman, Katy McDevitt, Dawn Busato

Triumph Books: Mitch Rogatz,
Siobhan Drummond

Opus Productions would like to recognize and thank the writers who contributed the feature essays for this book:
JIM COLEMAN Teeder Kennedy; Cyclone Taylor • TRENT FRAYNE Johnny Bower; Foster Hewitt; Red Horner; Red Storey
GARE JOYCE Jean Béliveau; Guy Lafleur; Brad Park • JIM TAYLOR Bobby Hull; Gordie Howe

Opus Productions would like to extend special thanks
to the Honoured Members of the Hockey Hall of Fame, who have so kindly cooperated
in sharing with us their stories, lives and legends for this book: Jean Béliveau, Johnny Bower, Red Horner,
Gordie Howe, Bobby Hull, Teeder Kennedy, Guy Lafleur, Brad Park and Red Storey.

Opus Productions would like to thank the following for their invaluable assistance:
Pat Armstrong, B.C. Sports Hall of Fame and Museum; Andrew Castell; Jerry Eberts; Jan Fridrik; Andrew Gardner;
Linda Goodman, Gayle Robson, Supreme Graphics; Nora Hague, Anette McConnell, McCord Museum; Jane Humphreys;
Mac Photographics; Dan Mikolay; Lisa Morrison; Emma and Hadley Obodiac; Jean Roy; Ed Sweeney; Fred Jr. and John Taylor.

Facing page: A keen sportsman, Lord Stanley embraced Canada's winter pastimes while serving as the governor-general.
Back double endsheet: A Hall of Fame scoring chance: "Mr. Hockey" Gordie Howe (left) fires at Terry Sawchuk in the Leafs' goal, 1965–66.